Albania

Getting around in Peshkopi

Albania

BY DAVID K. WRIGHT

Enchantment of the World
Second Series

Children's Press®

A Division of Grolier Publishing

NEW YORK   LONDON   HONG KONG   SYDNEY
DANBURY, CONNECTICUT

Consultant: Sami Repisti, Ph.D.

Please note: All statistics are as up-to-date as possible at the time of publication.

Library of Congress Cataloging-in-Publication Data

Wright, David K.
     Albania / David K. Wright.
          p. cm. — (Enchantment of the world. Second series)
          Includes bibliographical references and index.
  Summary: Describes the geography, plants, animals, history, economy, language,
          religions, culture, sports, arts, and people of Albania.
          ISBN 0-516-20468-8
          1. Albania—Juvenile literature. [1. Albania.] I. Title. II. Series.
          DR943.W75   1997
          949.65—dc21   97-4973
                                                                         CIP
                                                                         AC

To Albanian-Americans,
for their
contributions to both countries

Contents

A colorful Durrës dusk

The Land of the Eagle

The people who live in Albania call their country Shqipëria—The Land of the Eagle. The flag of Albania shows a black, two-headed eagle on a field of bright red. Imagine this ancient symbol as representing the two major branches of Albanians—the Ghegs and the Tosks. They live in a rugged part of Europe known as the Balkan Peninsula. Sometimes this area has found itself shut off from important events on the rest of the continent and the world. At other times, storms and stress in the Balkans have been front-page news.

YOU MIGHT LOOK AT A MAP OF EUROPE AND THINK THAT Albania, located between Greece and Italy, has always been in the middle of things. And, after all, ancestors of the Albanians, known as Illyrians, had a thriving civilization at least as early as the Greeks did—and even earlier than the Romans.

Yet much of European history has passed Albania by. This fact is puzzling, since many armies have crossed the country on their way to and from great battles and some historians consider lands around the Mediterranean Sea oases of civilization. Ancient or modern, however, Albania has not often been the focus of world attention.

Albania's Geography

Albania is a mountainous nation about the size of the state of Maryland—11,000 square miles (28,500 sq km). This small Balkan country is a land of green hills and lofty mountains separated by narrow valleys, rivers, and streams. It is divided into twenty-six districts, many of them named after nearby cities, rivers, lakes, or mountains. The country's highest points are in the eastern mountains and in the north, where the snowcapped peaks of the southern Alps tower over the landscape. The lowest point is at sea level all along the coast.

About three-quarters of Albania is mountainous or hilly.

Albania is bordered by the Adriatic Sea on the west, by Greece on the southeast, and by Macedonia (a former Yugoslav republic) on the east. Kosovo (an autonomous region of the Yugoslav republic, Serbia) lies to the northeast and Montenegro (a republic of Yugoslavia) to the northwest.

The country's coastline measures 225 miles (362 km). Italy is only 35 miles (56 km) away across the Strait of Otranto, a narrow passage between the Adriatic and Ionian Seas. The Adriatic and Ionian Seas combine to form a large arm of the Mediterranean Sea. The Mediterranean has been a seaway since ancient times, when people set out to explore the world.

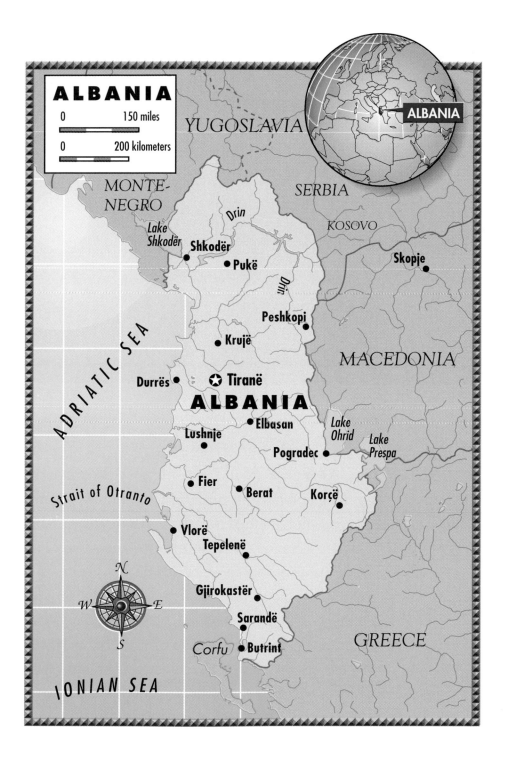

Geopolitical map
of Albania

The city of Sarandë lies along Albania's southern coast.

Today in Albania

At the moment, Albanians are trying to improve their lives by building a democratic society after a rigid Communist government kept the people subdued for forty-eight years—from 1944 to 1992. If democracy and modernization are to succeed, the Ghegs, Tosks, and others must continue to accept each other's cultural and religious differences.

Highland Ghegs outnumber lowland Tosks by about two to one. The two groups get along because of a shared past and because they speak slightly different dialects of the same language. The Albanian tongue has fascinated researchers for years—there is no other language on earth quite like it.

Several things are working in favor of Albanian citizens. First, they are eager to improve themselves. They know the standard of living is much higher in other European countries and they badly want to catch up. Thousands of men have left Albania to labor in fields and factories all over Europe. They save the money they earn so that they can return to their homeland and provide for their families. Most Albanians can read, and many have learned English, French, German, or Italian in school or by listening to the radio.

Albanians, such as this young seamstress, are eager for opportunities to improve their standard of living.

A History of Besa and Feuds

Muslim or Christian, Gheg or Tosk, Albanians have a reputation for being gracious hosts and fierce enemies. For centuries, they have believed in *besa*, which—roughly translated—means "pledge" or "word of honor." Among other things, it describes how a host should treat a guest. Guests in an Albanian home are considered to be under the protection of the host family. Whoever shows up at the door of an Albanian home gets the best food, the seat nearest the fireplace, and the most comfortable bed.

Over the centuries, however, Albanians have literally taken to the hills when foreigners invade. Albanian history is full of tales of small bands of ill-equipped farmers who overpowered large forces of Turks or Italians or Germans. The only road to victory for an invading army was to stay out of the highlands and concentrate on controlling the larger towns and agricultural areas.

Unfortunately, rural people have sometimes been tough on each other too. Feuds between individuals and clans have resulted in many murderous battles and forced some men to hide in the mountains for years to avoid being hunted down by their enemies. Happily, such feuds have greatly decreased in recent times.

Understanding the Past

The mountains are now being explored by outsiders who are fascinated with how these Albanians, cut off from the modern world, are reacting. Shepherds and farm families have lived there for generations, virtually untouched by events elsewhere in the country or the world. Not even the Communists were able to alter the beliefs of the mountain people.

Outsiders are understandably intrigued by Albania. The country provides a major source of electrical power, but its greatest economic potential is its people and scenic landscape. Both are relatively unspoiled, which should draw tourists from all over the world to the small Balkan country.

Europeans in particular are interested in the last country to emerge from behind the Iron Curtain of Communism. After

In Albania's mountain villages, life is difficult. Here, a woman does her laundry in the wintry outdoors.

all, Albania's Communist government allowed few visitors. For example, when the Scottish national soccer team was playing an important game in Albania, even the Scottish sportswriters were refused admittance.

Today, Albania is on its way to being a great tourist destination. The south offers the sandy beaches and sunny skies of the Albanian Riviera. Italians and other Europeans enjoy Albania's coastline, where sheer cliffs plunge into the Adriatic Sea. And the Albanian Alps are ideal for skiing and other winter sports. Elsewhere, tourists may visit historic sites—churches, mosques, and ancient Roman ruins. Albania hopes to develop its beaches, mountains, and historic areas with the care they deserve.

The government must make sure that the Albanian people benefit from tourism, however. If money from foreign visitors is used to benefit its citizens, Albania will truly have entered the modern world.

The Illyrian ruins of Apollonia near the city of Fier

The Mountains

Approximately 70 percent of Albania is mountainous. In addition to being difficult to farm, mountains make the weather harsh and unpredictable. Providing a shady, blue-gray background to many towns and cities, the towering peaks are loved for their beauty but loathed for the hardship they cause.

The climate on the southernmost coast of Albania—the Ionian Riviera—is mostly hot and arid.

THESE MOUNTAINS HAVE GREATLY INFLUENCED THE NATION'S history. The Ghegs, one of the two Albanian language groups, live in the northern mountains where the rugged peaks and hillsides have kept them isolated. Their countrymen to the south, the Tosks, have been overrun several times by invaders. Ghegs have been relatively free from outsiders because their homeland is so barren, cold, craggy, and remote.

The country's northern peaks rise up to 8,840 feet (2,694 m) above sea level. They mark the area where the Alps run in a north-south direction into the country. These limestone peaks have little vegetation, in part because they have been grazed for centuries by livestock. The country's highest peak, Mount Korab, rises 9,025 feet (2,751 m) in the central uplands.

The lowlands along Albania's coast are marked by small mountain ranges and hills.

Geographical Features

Longest River: Drin River, 175 miles (282 km)

Deepest Lake: Lake Ohrid, 941 feet (287 m)

Highest Elevation: Mount Korab, 9,025 feet (2,751 m)

Lowest Elevation: Sea level

Greatest Annual Precipitation: Albanian Alps, more than 100 inches (2.5 m) per year

Lowest Annual Precipitation: Eastern border, less than 30 inches (76 cm) per year

Longest Shared Border: With Greece, 175 miles (282 km)

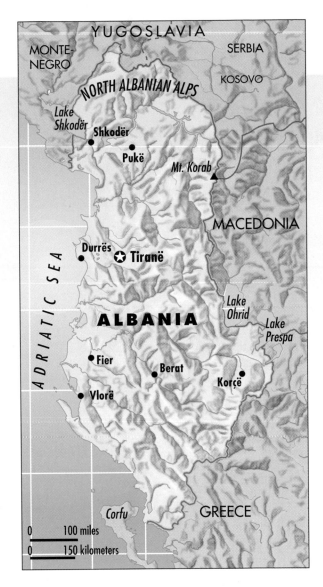

Until recently, swamps in these areas bred malarial mosquitoes, but most swampy sites near the sea have been filled in and are framed by pretty seaside cliffs. Miles of beautiful beaches stretch along the southernmost part of the coast—the Ionian Riviera.

Rivers and Lakes

The longest river in Albania, the Drin, flows only 175 miles (282 km) from its source to its mouth. Like the other major rivers, it runs roughly westward into the sea. The lone exception is the Lim, which flows north and eventually joins the legendary Danube River.

Topographical map of Albania

Much of Albania's power is generated by hydroelectric dams.

Opposite: **Albania has yet to develop into a strong industrial country. In the past, the country has made its living mostly from farming.**

Rivers can become raging torrents in the spring when snow melts in the highlands. Their steep plunging waters power machinery that runs the nation's electrical system. Albania produces so much electricity from its surging waters, it sells the extra power to its neighbors, though summers are so dry that rivers in lowland valleys may be no more than a trickle.

The country has three wonderful, unpolluted lakes along its borders. The shores of Lake Shkodër, also called Lake Scutari, are shared with Montenegro in the north. Lakes Ohrid and Prespa in the east mark the borders of Albania, Greece, and Macedonia. The Greek and Macedonian shores may be thick with tourists, but the Albanian sides of the lakes are still undeveloped. The largest lake entirely within the country is in Lurë National Park, northeast of Tiranë.

Farmers and owners of livestock all over Albania divert rivers and streams for their own use. Orchards have sophisticated irrigation systems, while farm ponds are filled through a series of ditches and dams made of earth.

Snows and Siroccos

Albania has four distinct seasons. Winds from Europe move south along the mountains, bringing cold, often snowy, northern winters. In contrast, the winds off the Mediterranean Sea keep coastal regions mild. Areas between the beaches and peaks get warm winds in summer and inland winds the rest of the year. Precipitation averages 55 inches (140 cm), little of which falls in summer. The coast gets the least rain; the mountains get the most.

Around the Mediterranean, winds from Europe meet winds from Africa. Coastal breezes move back and forth into the interior, and a hot, hazy, North African wind called the sirocco hits the south periodically each winter.

Albania's climate cannot be blamed for the country's lack of farmland—the soil has been depleted from centuries of farming, grazing, and runoff. Only about 20 percent of the

Terracing

Some crops that grow in Albania are possible because the steep slopes have been terraced to prevent soil erosion. A terraced hillside (above) looks like a great staircase. This farming technique allows farmers to grow fruits, grains, and vegetables on land that otherwise might be used only for pasture. During the Communist years, when vast terracing projects were undertaken, all Albanian adults were ordered into the countryside to work on fields and railroads. Unfortunately, many parts of northern and eastern Albania are too steep for terraced farming.

land is suitable for crops. Permanent crops such as trees make up only about 4 percent of the total, while meadows and pastures cover almost 40 percent.

Natural Resources

A European banker recently summed up Albania's natural resources this way: "A little chrome, a little nickel. But a fantastic landscape." However, the country has large deposits of coal, though they are sometime hard to reach and the quality is uneven. Oil and gas deposits also may become profitable as

This worker mines chromium, one of Albania's most important natural resources.

Monuments to Fear

From north to south, thousands of ugly concrete bunkers dot Albania's landscape. They were constructed everywhere in the 1960s and 1970s, when the Communist government was convinced the nation would be invaded. Some bunkers have been filled with soil and others are used for farm storage. No one has invaded Albania since World War II, more than fifty years ago.

the country develops. Other minerals found in some quantity include copper, iron, and bitumen (a coal product). In addition, Albania's chromium, with its high metal content, is among the world's best.

During the final years of the Communist regime in Albania, several other natural resources were explored. Phosphorite was mined to produce fertilizer, and such metals as lead, bauxite, and zinc were found in encouraging quantities. Unfortunately, little was done in any of the mining sites to preserve topsoil or otherwise conserve the land for alternative uses. It will take centuries for some of these mined areas to recover.

Animals and Plants

In earlier times, when feuds were common, almost every farmer owned and carried a long-barreled gun of one sort or another to protect himself and his family. As a result, wildlife populations have been greatly reduced, though there are now strict hunting seasons.

Particularly in the less populated north and northeast, foxes and wolves still roam the countryside, and wild pigs and boars are seen on occasion. The small deer called chamois are increasingly threatened as forests are cut for firewood and construction. A few bears can be found in the highlands, though their numbers are small.

O NCE PLENTIFUL, EAGLES—ALBANIA'S NAMESAKE—ARE now found mainly in remote mountains. Shooting an eagle is as unthinkable in Albania today as it is in the United States or Canada.

The most abundant wildlife in Albania is seen along the coast each winter. Thousands of birds such as swallows from all across northern Europe migrate to this sunny stretch of salt water, sand, and rock. They nest, feed on fish, and breed in preparation for their return journey to as far away as the Arctic Circle. Local species such as pelicans, gulls, and other seabird varieties live along the coast the year around.

The Chamois

Is it a goat? Is it a deer? It's actually a goatlike deer known as the chamois (pronounced SHAM-ee). It stands only about 30 inches (76 cm) at the shoulder and weighs 50 to 100 pounds (23 to 46 kg). The adult chamois has small, hollow horns that curl sharply backward at the tips. But it is the skin of the chamois that has made it famous—and threatened.

The chamois skin, which is very soft, is used to make clothing and polishing cloths. The soft, light-tan leather is taken from the deer only in the summer after the animal sheds it thick winter underfur. The deer live along the snowline, traveling in small herds and feeding on mountain herbs and flowers. In the winter, chamois eat pine shoots.

Today, chamois herds are so few in number that they are protected by laws. Because the chamois is so shy and lives in such remote places, few Albanians have ever seen this tiny, fascinating creature.

Albania has never had a vast fleet of fishing boats, but its waters provide the most diverse wildlife. Hundreds of species of fish thrive in the coastal waters along with everything else aquatic, from octopuses to dolphins. Freshwater fish include river and lake trout, and the country's three major lakes are home to some "living fossils"—varieties of fish found nowhere else.

Lake Ohrid, one of Albania's largest lakes, is the center of much wildlife.

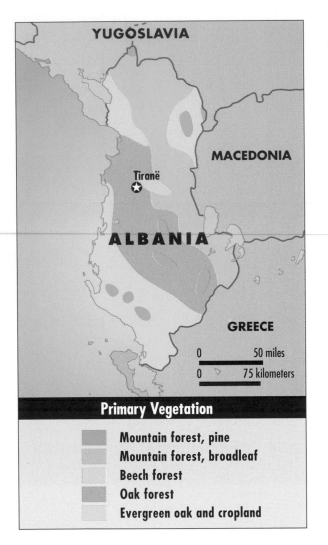

Map of Albania's vegetation

MACEDONIA

Tiranë

ALBANIA

GREECE

0   50 miles

0   75 kilometers

Primary Vegetation

- Mountain forest, pine
- Mountain forest, broadleaf
- Beech forest
- Oak forest
- Evergreen oak and cropland

Vegetation

Thanks to its mountains and its location, Albania is home to an incredible variety of plant life, too. Not many small countries can boast of high-altitude pine trees at one end and tropical palms at the other.

Unfortunately, every kind of tree, from the leafiest palm to the loftiest pine, is in danger today in Albania. With the collapse of Communism in 1991, a mix of vengeance and need overcame many Albanians. They cut down trees everywhere, primarily for warmth but also for spite. Towns and cities once graced with tree-lined roads were left with the withered stumps. Because gasoline is cheap and available, it is sometimes used in homes to make stubborn logs burn.

As late as 1970, 40 percent of Albania's land was forested. That figure may now be cut in half. Common trees include oaks, which are sometimes stunted in the lowlands, with a variety of palm trees in the extreme south. In higher elevations, beeches and pines are the mainstay of the remaining forests. Other northern trees include chestnuts, while willows are common in river valleys.

Albania has more than 3,000 varieties of plants and herbs, the most common being a Mediterranean shrub called the maquis. Hundreds of flowers blossom in Alpine meadows during the summer months. A few of these flowers provide fragrant essences used in perfumes and flavorings.

If eagles are the glory of Albania's wildlife, fruit-bearing trees are its most impressive lowland vegetation. Olive trees yield oil that is the basis for much of the country's food and provide fruit, too. And wherever olives grow there are figs, since the two have similar soil, water, and climatic needs. Carefully tended grapevines can be seen on the fertile hills. Citrus trees such as oranges or lemons are common in the south, while plums are grown with care in several parts of the country. The southern tip of Albania is warm enough to support banana trees.

In the southern part of the country, the vegetation is tropical.

A Mediterranean Land of History

One of the best things about Albania is its visible history. The ancient Illyrians, Greeks, Romans, and many others left fascinating evidence around the country. Few nations can boast of so many undisturbed historical sites.

LITTLE IS KNOWN ABOUT THE FIRST PEOPLE TO LIVE IN Albania—some 12,000 years ago—or about the people who lived along the southern coast in 5000 B.C. The early residents could have come from present-day Austria or Russia, or anywhere in between. The first people identified by scientists were the Pelasgians. They were forebears of the Illyrians—the ancestors of modern Albanians.

The Illyrians soon mingled with early Greeks. It is likely that the two groups traded with each other, and the Illyrians may have worked the land while the Greeks fished and sailed the seas. By about 500 B.C., Illyrians had established cities in several sites across present-day Albania and beyond. Ancient writings indicate that the Illyrian kingdom spread into parts of what are now Kosovo, Macedonia, and Montenegro.

Conquering the Illyrians

Philip II of Macedonia, the father of Alexander the Great, conquered the Illyrians in 359 B.C. Alexander's mother came from Epirus, then a part of Illyria. The warrior king included many Illyrians in his far-flung army. Around 300 B.C., Illyria's King Glaucius made an alliance with Rome. The Romans called the Illyrians *Albani*, which evolved into *Albania*.

Alexander the Great: Conqueror and Hero

Alexander the Great (left) lived to be only thirty-three years old. Yet, even before his death, legends preceded and followed him, from the rugged Balkan Peninsula into Asia and back to Egypt and Greece.

Alexander was born in 356 B.C. to King Philip II and Queen Olympias of Macedonia. His mother was from Epirus, now part of Albania. The boy's father was an ambitious man who wanted his son to be an educated warrior. So while Philip was busy conquering foreign lands, he saw to it that the great philosopher Aristotle and other scholars taught young Alexander.

The boy quickly discovered what was expected of him. While his father was away, Alexander was left in charge of the kingdom. When he was only sixteen years old, he led his father's warriors in defeating foreign soldiers who staged a sneak attack. One year later, he helped his father defeat an army from the Greek states.

Philip was assassinated (right) when Alexander was twenty years old. The young king quickly had rivals to the throne killed, then rallied Macedonians and Greeks in preparation for a huge invasion of Asia. Almost simultaneously, he defeated a horde from what is now Europe and an invading army from Illyria.

Persia (a large part of the eastern Mediterranean at the time) was a kingdom of great riches. Alexander's army began the Persian expedition in 334 B.C., marching through Turkey. Wherever the soldiers went, they were followed by people who built new cities and set up Macedonian laws and ways of living. Alexander welcomed local people who accepted his rule and killed many of those who did not.

He conquered Persia by moving his huge force quickly from one place to another. When he could not beat a foe one way, he found another way. For example, the Persians had a large navy that allowed them to move troops in a hurry. Alexander captured all Persia's coastal cities, thus preventing the naval forces from obtaining food or water.

Still in his early twenties, Alexander conquered much of western Asia. He moved into lands even more rugged and barren than his native Macedonia, taking control of modern-day Iran, Iraq, and Syria. Turning westward in

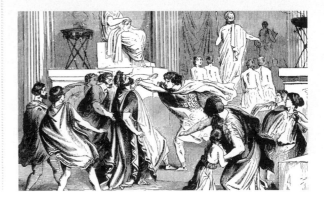

332 B.C., he led his victorious army into Egypt. Welcomed by the people there, he built the great city of Alexandria, a center for learning.

By the age of twenty-five, Alexander enjoyed a fame spread even more widely than his armies. One legend told of his encounter with the Gordian knot. An ancient prophecy said that the man who could untie the Gordian knot would conquer Asia. But this rope knot was said to be tied so tightly that no man could undo it. Alexander reportedly studied the knot, then hacked it to pieces with his sword!

Alexander defeated the Persians (right) and buried their general, Darius, with military honors. He then continued eastward into unexplored territory in central Asia. The army, composed of people from lands defeated by the Macedonians, moved through what is now Afghanistan. Snow and ice loomed as the men and their followers trudged through valleys surrounded by immense Himalayan peaks.

Hardship was constant. The army often ran low on food, and crossing deserts, they ran out of water. Alexander angered his own Macedonian warriors by killing one of their generals. Nevertheless, in the early summer of 327 B.C., the huge mass of soldiers invaded India, the setting of another legend. Alexander was told by one of his soldiers that there was nowhere left in the civilized world to conquer. He is said to have wept over the idea that no more battles could be won. But many of his men—thousands of miles from home in a hot, wet climate—threatened mutiny if Alexander did not return to Macedonia.

Alexander built several ships before leaving India and sent thousands of his warriors home in the wooden vessels. He himself marched with his foot soldiers all the way back to the Mediterranean. On the way, he checked on the cities he had founded. If they were badly run, he did not hesitate to replace those he had put in charge.

Alexander's last year was marked by his growing belief that he was a god and immortal. Perhaps he felt he could not be killed because he had twice recovered from serious battle wounds. Nevertheless, on June 13, 323 B.C., after eating a big meal and consuming a great deal of alcohol, Alexander died, probably of either food poisoning or intoxication.

The conqueror founded more than seventy cities. He made people realize there were major civilizations in far-flung places. Alexander also spread Greek education and ideas, holding together a huge and expanding kingdom by the sheer force of his personality. The reign of Alexander the Great was one of the most noted periods in the history of the world.

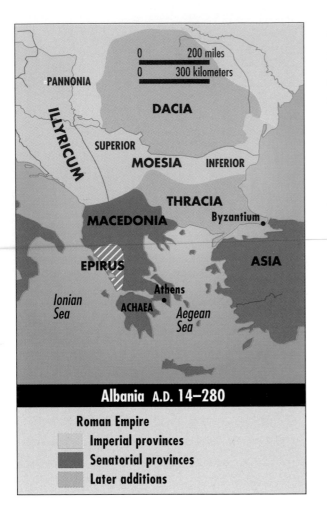

Albania A.D. 14–280

Roman Empire
- Imperial provinces
- Senatorial provinces
- Later additions

Albanians came under Roman rule in about 165 B.C., and, along with the Romans some 200 years later, accepted Christianity.

Roman rulers later decided that the Balkan Peninsula was part of Rome's eastern empire, despite its nearness. So Albanians were governed by Romans and others living in the city of Constantinople. Today, the Romans' most lasting monuments are the well-built roads used by their legions to march through Albania on their way to battle.

From about the A.D. 300s, many warlike peoples swept across the Balkan Peninsula, including Goths, Huns, Avars, Lombards, Serbs, Croats, and Bulgars. These people probably recruited sturdy Albanian troops as they advanced to and from Italy, Greece, and elsewhere.

A Church Divided

In 1054, the Christian Church split in two over matters of faith. One division became the Roman Catholic Church, headed by men who called themselves popes and lived in Rome's Vatican City. The other division became the Orthodox Church, led by patriarchs based in the Byzantine Empire city of Constantinople. Most Ghegs in the north fol-

In the A.D. 300s, the Huns overran the Balkans.

lowed Rome while most Tosks in the south looked to the Orthodox leadership for guidance.

However, it wasn't long before the Muslim Turks overran Asia Minor, including Constantinople, which greatly affected the Orthodox Church. Roman Catholic Pope Urban II called in 1095 for a crusade, or holy war, to restore the Holy Land (present-day Israel) to Christian rule. This brought more change to Albania, as crusading foreigners passed through the land headed for battle far to the east. A few French, German, and Scottish crusaders married and remained in Albania.

In the center of Tiranë stands a monument of Skenderbeg on horseback.

helping the ragtag Albanian and Hungarian force to defeat the Turks—for the time being.

Skenderbeg abandoned not only the Turks but also the religion of Islam. He returned to Christianity as a Roman Catholic, thus securing the assistance of the pope. Rounding up fellow princes from Albania, he declared a crusade against the mighty Ottoman Empire.

As commander in chief of this League of Princes and their troops, Skenderbeg beat back Turkish forces trying to enter

Albania up to twenty-four times between 1444 and 1468. In addition to leading tough soldiers, who were often outnumbered, Skenderbeg successfully sought arms and money from fellow-Christians elsewhere in Europe.

He traveled to Rome and other Italian cities, making friends and receiving many religious titles and blessings. Pope Calixtus III named him Captain General of the Holy See—in effect, the commander-in-chief of the Christian world. When Skenderbeg's forces defeated those of Turkish Sultan Murad II in 1450, his name was known all over Europe as "the defender of Christendom."

Unfortunately, no one could rally forces like Skenderbeg. He died in 1468 and, ten years later, Ottoman forces captured one Albanian city after another. Many Albanians fled the country. Those who stayed were forced to convert from Christianity to Islam.

The Turks

The 400-plus years in which Turkey ruled Albania were marked by repeated attempts to convert the population to Islam. When the Turks took over, the country was divided between the more numerous followers of Eastern Orthodox Christianity and Roman Catholicism.

With the passing years, however, Albanians were forced to follow Islam in order to cultivate land or get work. The local people often made a public display of being Muslim, but privately worshiped as Christians. Yet, by the dawn of the 1900s, nearly 70 percent of Albania's population truly considered

The Code of Leke Dukagjini: A Book of Values

Though Skenderbeg has been the national hero of Albania for centuries, one of his comrades had at least as much impact on the country. That person was Leke Dukagjini, who lived from 1410 to 1481. No one is sure of Dukagjini's ancestry; he may have been Italian, or he could have been descended from a long line of native Albanians, like Skenderbeg. Regardless, his northern family was wealthy and well known and he was a close friend of the commander-in-chief.

The period during which Dukagjini lived was marked by many attempted invasions from Turkey. The powerful Muslim Ottoman Empire was at its height, and Turkish rulers did not want the small Christian state of Albania causing them problems. To combat the foreign influence, Albanian nobles such as Dukagjini promised the people reforms. These reforms changed the country from a society ruled by nobles to one ruled by *kuvendi*—councils of large clans or tribes.

To influence the people and to bring order during a hectic time, Dukagjini assembled a book of laws. He did not make up the laws, but combined ancient rules used by Illyrians with Albanian, Greek, Roman, and other laws and ways of living. The book became known as the *Kanun* or *The Code of Leke Dukagjini*.

Large parts of Albania took Dukagjini's book to heart. After the Ottoman Empire overpowered much of Albania, the people sought even more comfort in the book of laws. It told how people were supposed to live, no matter who was in charge of the country.

People reading the book today are often amazed at the good sense found in the code. The rules cover the church, marriage, family, private property, honor, judicial law, and more. For example, "If a servant is displeasing to his master, the latter may dismiss him, but may not abuse him verbally or lay hands on him." Or, in a display of the famous Albanian hospitality, "The guest occupies the place of honor at the table."

Other rules were designed to make life easier. Everyone living in a village had to participate in running the village, for example. And there were rules about how things should be made: "A public highway must be broad enough so that a horse with its load and an ox with its yoke may (both) pass."

On the other hand, rules about murder and vengeance indicate that medieval Albanian society was violent. For example, there are statements explaining how a murderer should leave the body of his victim. Rules on revenge for all kinds of wrongs run through the book. And sadly, women and children were not always well treated.

With all its faults, however, *The Code of Leke Dukagjini* has been of immense value down through the centuries. It has given all the Albanians something in common besides language. The fact that the Turks grumbled about local laws shows the code was working all along. The fact that Albanian Communists also grumbled about the code shows that the Communists were equally insensitive to the people's wants and needs.

themselves Muslims. The years of Turkish occupation had a profound effect.

Albanians who became Muslims often achieved great success in the Ottoman Empire, either as soldiers or in government. They were accepted and trusted, serving as generals and prime ministers. One, Kara Mahmud Pasha Bushati, suspected that an alliance with Emperor Napoleon Bonaparte of France could result in enlarging his territory. Bushati successfully attacked nearby Montenegro in 1785 because it was an ally of Bonaparte's enemy, Russia. The Albanian leader was later named governor of northern Albania by the Turks.

Despite having occupied Albania for hundreds of years, the Turks did not always know peace. An Albanian leader named Ali Pasha, born in the town of Tepelenë, was hunted down and assassinated by the Turks in 1822 for preaching to his countrymen that Albania should be independent. Pasha's movement encouraged the Greeks, who staged a war for independence in 1821–1829.

The Balkans, 1800

In 1830, more than 1,000 Albanian leaders from various towns and cities demanded to meet and discuss their grievances with the Ottoman general who ran the country. When talk turned to independence, the Turkish leader immediately killed half of them. By 1835, the Turks

Albanian leader Ali Pasha was killed by the Turks in 1822.

had divided the country into the provinces of Iannina, Monastir, and Shkodër, in part to keep Albanians isolated from each other.

Albanians today, whether Muslim or Christian, say the period of Turkish occupation was hard. "The only thing

Turkey brought to us was the kitchen," said an old woman. She meant that Turkish cooks and their Mediterranean diets were superior to native cooks and their diets.

There was enough freedom by 1861 so that the first school to teach in the Albanian language opened in Shkodër. It was operated by Roman Catholic clergy.

The Ottoman Decline

The Balkans received help from an unexpected source during the winter of 1877–1878. Russian troops, equipped with modern weapons, defeated a force of Ottoman soldiers in the most important battle of the Russo-Turkish War. That battle told Europe and the world that the Turkish empire was weak—"the sick man of Europe." To the Albanians, it meant that they might receive support in their bid to be free.

The Treaty of San Stefano in 1878 came as a blow to Albania. Without consulting anyone, Russia took Albania from the Turks and split it among Russian allies. The country was divided among Bulgaria, Greece, Montenegro, and Serbia. Austro-Hungary and Great Britain prevented the treaty from being enforced, but the Albanians realized they could not expect much help in their fight for freedom.

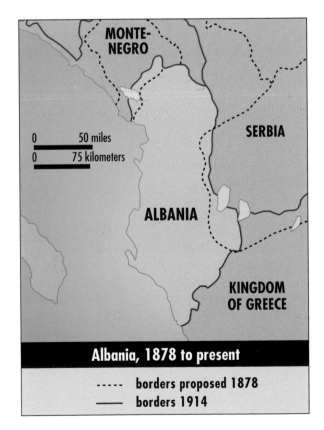

Albania, 1878 to present
- - - - - borders proposed 1878
———— borders 1914

Insurrection in northern Albania in the 1880s

By the late 1800s, many people in Albania knew what they had been missing. The Industrial Revolution had begun in Europe in the late 1700s, and countries such as England, France, and Germany were now wealthy nations filled with well-fed, well-dressed, well-educated people. Albanians believed that the Turkish presence prevented them from enjoying such progress.

The Turks reacted to this belief by killing several Albanian leaders and banning Albanian-language books. By 1899, Turkish forces could no longer control the resentment in southern Albania. And in 1908, a number of Albanian teachers bravely met and chose to teach the Albanian language, using the Latin alphabet as standard for the country. Clearly, citizens wanted to be associated with western Europe rather than with eastern Europe or Asia.

Five hundred years of Turkish occupation ended for Albania on November 28, 1912. Hatred boiled over in a widespread revolt in Skopje, now a city in Macedonia, and soon spread throughout the Balkan Peninsula. Unable to put down the Albanian desire for independence, Turkish forces withdrew and a national government was proclaimed in the city of Vlorë. It would be led by a man named Ismail Qemali.

The First Balkan War

Freedom for Albania came before the First Balkan War, a war that saw the Turks lose almost all their remaining Balkan territory. Unfortunately, the treaty that ended the war in 1913 was put together in London by people who had little knowledge of the Albanian situation. Consequently, they created new boundaries that placed nearly half of all Albanians outside their own country. Albanians went to bed in one nation—their own—and woke up in Montenegro or Serbia or Greece. It is no wonder that the Second Balkan War erupted shortly afterward.

The Treaty of Bucharest ended the Second Balkan War. This time, the "Great Powers" recognized Albania as an independent state. However, the treaty makers sent a German, Prince Wilhelm of Wied, to run the country. Massive unrest soon forced Wilhelm and his government to return to Germany. Meanwhile, a Serb assassinated a member of the Austro-Hungarian royal family—an event that led to the outbreak of World War I in 1914.

World at War

During World War I, France, Great Britain, Italy, and Russia took on Austria-Hungary and Germany in a massive slaughter. Albania was occupied by Austria-Hungary, and at the end of

Ahmed Bey Zogu, known as King Zog, ruled Albania from 1925 to 1939.

the war the Italian army controlled most of Albania. French, Greek, and Serbian forces were in charge of the rest of the country. Albanian leaders wanted their independence to be a topic of the 1919 Paris Peace Conference, but they were denied any sort of representation.

Meanwhile, Greek and Serb soldiers seized control in most Albanian cities as a struggle for the country began among Greece, Italy, and Serbia. Many Albanians took to the hills, ambushing Serbian patrols and generally making life miserable for any uniformed foreigner. The Treaty of Paris in 1919 divided Albania between Greece and Italy, among others. Albanian leaders met, rejected the treaty, warned of bloodshed, and in 1920 created a national legislature.

Independence and Admission

Leaders moved to the city of Tiranë, proclaiming it Albania's capital. At the same time, Albanian guerrilla fighters forced Italy to withdraw its troops and abandon its claims to Albanian territory. Europe must have been impressed with Albanian determination—in December 1920, Albania was admitted as an independent country to the League of Nations (an international association similar to the United Nations).

That admission was a high point in the country's history, but several low points occurred shortly afterward. Montenegro and Serbia were part of a newly created union of states called *Yugoslavia* (Land of the South Slavs). Serbia had always wanted a seaport, and Albania seemed the most likely site. One of the benefits of Albania's League of Nations membership became evident when Serbs and Montenegrins invaded: The League of Nations successfully ordered them to leave.

Ahmed Bey Zogu

Albanians knew that their hard-won independence was not to be taken for granted. In 1921, the Popular Party formed a government headed by Xhafer Ypi. His minister of internal affairs, Ahmed Bey Zogu, took over as prime minister in 1922. At the same time, the Albanian Orthodox Church was established.

Zogu was a smart politician. During an attempt to overthrow his government in 1922, he persuaded the British ambassador to tell the rioters to go home. Zogu then destroyed the small group of rebel forces who refused to leave, giving the impression that Zogu and his government had triumphed over a huge mob.

Important events happening elsewhere also affected Albania. Mussolini, the first Fascist dictator, came to power in Italy. He resented the fact that Albanians had forced Italian troops to withdraw from their country a few years earlier, so he urged his supporters to seek another foothold on the Balkan Peninsula. Meanwhile, an Albanian-American named Fan S. Noli was stirring things up among Albanian peasants. After an unsuccessful attempt on his life, Zogu fled the country in 1924. Another group took over the capital of Tiranë, with Noli as prime minister.

Fan Noli's Brief Reign

Fan Noli made his home in the United States but was Albanian by birth. He was also a writer, a historian, and a bishop in the Albanian Orthodox Church. The Boston, Massachusetts, resident promoted democratic government in Albania and returned to his native land to see what he could do. He had the people on his side but was opposed by landowners in the south and highland chieftains in the north. These traditional feudal leaders were worried and suspicious about giving the people control.

Zogu was worried, too. He made secret promises to Yugoslavia and Italy, then called on Albania's army to throw out the democratic government Noli and his people were trying to form. Zogu returned to Tiranë in December 1924 and began to destroy the democratic parliament that had been set up. Noli fled across the Strait of Otranto to Italy and Zogu resumed power.

In return for their support, Zogu gave the Yugoslavs a monastery on Lake Ohrid in Albania's highlands. Italians were given a defense treaty that would hand them eventual control of Albania. Zogu accepted a bundle of Italian money and was encouraged to call himself king rather than president.

"King of All Albanians"

That was the title preferred by Zogu, popularly known as King Zog I. Intelligent and able, he nevertheless made rash decisions, started up and closed government departments at will, and established a monarchy backed by tough police. But the thing for which his people could not forgive him was his willingness to let Italians gradually take over the country.

In Zog's defense, he tried to bring Albania into the twentieth century. He came down hard on feuding clans, feeling that revenge and bloodshed had no place in a modern soci-

Opposite: **Fan S. Noli, an Orthodox bishop-turned-politician, served as Albania's prime minister for only six months.**

King Zog with former countess Geraldine of Hungary after the royal nuptials in 1938

Albanian troops on alert in Tiranë after Italy threatened invasion in 1939

ety. He did little to improve the country's poor economy, but he did manage to get things going for a brief period. Then the worldwide depression of the early 1930s made the average Albanian as poor and wretched as ever.

For Albania, World War II began in April 1939. Zog threw one of Mussolini's friends out of Albania, and the Italian dictator made a list of outrageous demands in return, including control of Albania's finances and armed forces, and the recruiting of Fascists in the country. When King Zog rejected the demands, some 60,000 Italian troops massed at a number of Italy's ports, waiting to board ships that would carry them across the short stretch of sea to Albania.

World War Begins

Italy invaded Albania on April 7, 1939, and Zog fled to Greece. With air power and modern weapons, the Italians took over the country with ease. Like the Turks before them, the Italians gained control of most cities and major roads.

On April 7, 1939, Italy invaded Albania. Here, Italian tanks advance through the port city of Durrës.

Only in the craggy mountains were Albanians free of the Italian presence.

Italy made the mistake of attacking Greece from southern Albania in 1940 and the well-armed Greeks began to push the Italians back toward the sea. German soldiers saved Mussolini's forces by driving south through the Balkans and attacking Greece. One year later, the Albanian Communist Party was founded. Enver Hoxha (pronounced HAW-juh) was named the party's first secretary.

Standing beneath a sign bearing the name of their hometown, partisan Albanians celebrate the end of German rule in November 1944.

Hundreds of small Albanian resistance groups harassed Italian and German soldiers throughout the war. Among them was a group of Communists who fell under Enver Hoxha's leadership.

Like Tito in Yugoslavia, Hoxha and his guerrilla fighters emerged from World War II determined to run the country. Organizing the National Liberation Movement even before the end of the war, the Communists gained control of the countryside as the Germans and Italians retreated. By November 1944, Communists were in control of Tiranë.

Communism Comes to Albania

With fellow-Communist Tito ruling Yugoslavia, Albanian Communists agreed to let the Slavs have the Kosovo region. This was decided despite the fact that most Kosovo residents were Albanian. Hoxha and his people were too busy persecuting their enemies inside Albania to disagree with Tito at that time. Fascists and democrats were branded as traitors and either imprisoned or executed. Simultaneously, in 1945, the state took over farms, industries, and transportation.

Then-general Enver Hoxha addresses a rally in 1945.

The losers were the large landowners who had always worked with whatever government was in power. Their farms were divided among the peasants, even though the peasants did not necessarily know much about agriculture. Several nations, most of them Communist, recognized the new government. The new rulers then took over all church property.

Hoxha, an admirer of the Soviet Union, began to run Albania as if it were a part of that giant land. He was named prime minister, foreign minister, defense minister, and commander-in-chief of the armed forces, thanks to a new constitution adopted by the People's Assembly. By the end of

Enver Hoxha: The Man Who Led Albania into Communism

What kind of man was Enver Hoxha? Albanians tell the story of a cabinet meeting where one of Hoxha's friends objected to the leader's plans. No one but a comrade from Hoxha's World War II days dared to argue with the president-prime minister. Hoxha ended the disagreement by pulling out a pistol and shooting his longtime friend dead on the spot!

The man who led Albania into Communism was born in the southern, Greek-influenced city of Gjirokastër in 1908. The son of a Muslim cloth merchant, Hoxha showed early promise and was given scholarships to a local French school. He went to France for additional schooling at the age of twenty-two.

Hoxha's education ended abruptly when the Albanian government canceled his scholarship. He stayed in Paris, wrote for political journals, and was hired as a clerk by Albanian government representatives in Brussels, Belgium. The Albanians read his stories in Communist newspapers and soon had him fired. He returned to Albania and became a schoolteacher.

World War II was terrible

for many people, but it gave the young teacher the break he needed. Hoxha was fired from his teaching position by Italian forces, so he moved to Tiranë and began to organize anti-Italian militants. His activities included starting the Albanian Communist Party in 1941 and helping circulate an anti-Fascist newspaper. Italian authorities wanted him dead and put a price on his head.

Tall and handsome, Hoxha was not always predictable. Even though Yugoslav Communists helped him put together the Communist Party in Albania, he did not trust them. However, he gained the confidence of the British and the Americans, who dropped weapons to Hoxha's forces in their battles against Italian and German troops. He was courageous in battle and a convincing public speaker.

When World War II ended in 1945, Hoxha's Communists were stronger than the guerrilla groups who supported democracy or the backers of Zog, the former king. Hoxha's government was recognized in 1945 by Britain, France, the Soviet Union, and the United States, and women voting for the first time chose this man. His new party gained control of the country in a fair election and Hoxha became Albania's president, prime minister, and commander-in-chief.

His leadership was both good and bad. He greatly increased the number of persons who could read, including the aged. But he made virtual war on religion and religious leaders by closing Catholic schools and executing or imprisoning priests. Hoxha started a great many public-improvement projects, but he often forced the public to do the labor—after they had already put in a hard day's work.

Typical of this kind of thinking was the building of the nation's railroad system. Hoxha ordered thousands of people into the countryside to cut brush and trees, lay gravel beds, and place rails and ties. Many Albanians made a party of it, picnicking and playing music but getting little work done. He also built some 700,000 concrete bunkers for what he saw as the defense of Albania against invaders. They still litter the landscape—ugly and useless.

Hoxha kept Albania isolated for many years. He snubbed Yugoslavia in 1948, the Soviet Union in 1960, and China in 1976. As he aged, he fancied himself an author. His autobiography, *The Artful Albanian*, is entertaining if not entirely truthful. Enver Hoxha died of natural causes in 1985 at the age of seventy-six.

1946, Albania had severed relations with the United States and Great Britain, although both had supported Albania in World War II.

Hoxha was a stubborn man. He turned down money offered by the United States to help him repair wartime damage. The Albanian Communist Party voted in 1948 to merge Albania's economy and military forces with Yugoslavia. But when the Soviets denounced Yugoslavia that same year, Hoxha cut all ties with the Slavs. He idolized Soviet dictator Joseph Stalin and urged his people to do likewise.

During the late 1940s and early 1950s, Hoxha got rid of Communists who had any sympathy for Yugoslavia. He also imprisoned large numbers of religious leaders of all faiths and tore down churches and mosques. By the mid-1950s, Albania had become a founding member of Communism's mutual defense agreement, the Warsaw Pact.

Differences with the Soviets

Stalin died in 1953, and in 1956 Soviet leader Nikita Khrushchev publicly denounced Stalin for having killed or imprisoned millions of innocent Soviet citizens. This infuriated Hoxha, who corrected Khrushchev at a large Communist meeting. The Soviets tried to smooth things over by sending Albania huge amounts of aid and encouraging Eastern Europe and China to do the same.

Albania joined China in its growing dispute with the Soviet Union in the early 1960s. Relations between Albania and the Soviet Union unraveled. Albanian citizens felt the lack of aid from the Soviet Union and its Eastern European allies. China was unable to make up the difference, resulting in a jolt to Hoxha's economic plans. Despite all his planning, Hoxha's people lived no better than they had fifty years earlier.

Already the poorest people in Europe, the Albanians were now forced into a tough austerity program. Stores routinely ran out of even basic foods, such as flour to make bread. Buses sat idle when they broke down. To make the people feel better, Hoxha in 1966 restructured wage rates: almost everyone, from the lowliest shepherd to the most important factory manager, was paid about the same.

Albanian president Enver Hoxha, shown with Soviet premier Nikita Khrushchev in 1957, broke off relations with the Soviet Union in 1960.

SHOKU
MAO CE-DUN
PËR RININË DHE
PUNËN ME RININË

One of Enver Hoxha's strongest alliances was with Communist China and Chairman Mao. Pictured here is an Albanian translation of Mao's writings.

If the Albanian people prayed for some kind of miracle, they had to do it at home because in 1967 the state began a violent anti-religion campaign. Without warning, historic churches and mosques all over the country—many of them hundreds of years old—were bulldozed into rubble. Believers had to pray in silence as some 2,000 religious buildings were knocked down in 1967 alone.

The following year—1968—the Soviet Union squashed Czechoslovakia's attempt to break out of the Communist web. Hoxha not only condemned Soviet actions, he pulled Albania out of the Warsaw Pact. From that point on, Albania could not count on any other European Communist country for aid if it were attacked. Except for Red China, the small country was utterly friendless.

After Chairman Mao's death in 1976, Hoxha had unkind words for the Chinese too. One year later, he threw out of the armed forces many Albanians who had received Chinese military training. The Chinese cut off all economic and military aid to Albania in 1978.

Hard-Line Hoxha Bows Out

Suffering from a number of illnesses that would eventually take his life, Hoxha in 1980 chose Ramiz Alia as the next head of the Communist Party. As Albanians struggled to get enough to eat and keep a roof over their heads, Hoxha worked on his memoirs and consulted with his doctors. He died of natural causes in the spring of 1985, about two years after Alia assumed control of the country.

Alia realized that the rest of Europe was leaving Albania in the economic dust. He agreed to a series of pacts with Greece that would result in Albanian farm products and raw materials being shipped to the Greeks in exchange for consumer goods. The Greeks were among world leaders in shipping, which meant that Albanian goods had a potentially worldwide market.

The problem was that Albania used up virtually everything it managed to make or grow. Consequently, Alia announced in 1989 that the country would have to undergo radical changes in the economic system if it were to survive. The average Albanian already was well aware of the shortcomings in the economy. While

Ramiz Alia, Hoxha's hand-picked replacement, assumed power in 1980.

A Mediterranean Land of History **59**

After Ramiz Alia granted Albanians limited freedom in 1990, thousands of citizens, desperate to leave the country, took refuge at foreign embassies.

European Communism was crumbling in places such as East Germany, Hungary, and Poland, Albanians in Shkodër were rioting over lack of opportunity.

Alia established diplomatic relations with the United States and the Soviet Union. The Soviets were having problems, as Soviet states abandoned Communism and became individual countries. Before the eyes of the world, Communism in 1989 in Europe and western Asia was simply disappearing—almost overnight, after decades in power. Only Albania, among all European countries, clung to its Marxist past.

Communism Collapses

The summer of 1990 was crucial for Albania. The more government loosened the reins, the more freedom people demanded. For example, Albanians were at last allowed to leave their country. Many men immediately departed for Germany, Greece, Italy, and elsewhere to get work so they could send money back to their families. They left any way they could—in leaky boats or by hiking through snowy mountain passes.

Other laws were eased, including those covering criminal codes, courts, even freedom of worship. Young people, led by university students, courageously demonstrated against the government in Tiranë. Some 5,000 Albanians barged into foreign embassies in their nation's capital, demanding refuge. To ease the years of want, the government opened the door to foreign trade in August 1990.

With the end of 1990 came the end of Communism in Albania. Students called for an end to the dictatorship— they had seen and heard what European life was like from television and radio and they feared being left in the past. A multiparty system was created and the Albanian Democratic Party, the first opposition political party, came into being. A new constitution was drafted and, in 1991, elections were held.

A woman casts her vote in Albania's first free election since World War II.

Despite the election of many non-Communists in the 1991 elections, troubles continued for Albania. Anti-government demonstrators were gunned down in Shkodër in the spring of 1991. In retaliation, non-Communists in power abolished Sigurimi, Albania's dreaded secret police. Some 5,000 men hiked into Greece and 18,000 tried to get into Italy. Most of them were returned by the Italian government.

Sali Berisha, leader of the Albanian Democratic Party, won the first presidential election, held in the spring of 1992. He faced an economy and a country in ruins. To make matters worse, several former Communists were elected by people who believed the past had been better than the present. Berisha has aimed Albania in the right directions, selling off government-controlled property and joining a number of religious, governmental, and defense organizations.

Sali Berisha, Albania's first freely elected leader

By the spring of 1996, with new elections and a growing economy, Albanians appeared to be headed for a better way of life. A year later, however, the country was rocked by a popular—and violent—uprising after the collapse of investment companies in which Albanians had deposited their savings. Hundreds have been killed in the unrest.

No other European leader faces bigger challenges than Sali Berisha. Besides the lack of order in Albania, the neighboring Kosovo region is filled with desperate persons of Albanian descent who are in rebellion against Yugoslavia. These people are aware that Albania has no money to help them. But they are also aware that their home country is a useful warehouse for guns and for the drug trafficking that bankrolls their revolution. The Serbian government of Yugoslavia has a tough time keeping the lid on Kosovo, which is 90 percent ethnic Albanian.

The collapse of high-risk investment schemes brought violence and unrest to Albania. By March 1997, U.S. citizens had to be evacuated under protection of armed guards.

The Road to Democracy

Albania has been making big news since 1990, when it became the last European nation to throw off a Communist dictatorship. Since this tense yet hopeful step toward freedom, the country has been trying to adjust. It has not been easy— manufacturing, agriculture, trade, and government are all trying to catch up to the rest of Europe and the world. There are other problems as well.

THE BALKAN WAR RAGED INTO THE MIDDLE 1990S ALMOST on Albania's doorstep, and Albania itself has shaky relations with Serbia, one of the aggressors in the conflict. Differences with Greece, Macedonia, and Montenegro over human rights and other matters are also troubling. Italy and Albania do not always see eye to eye either, but they have developed good political and economic relations. For example, Italy has helped start a program to prevent organized crime in the new Albania.

Changing Times

Think about this: An Albanian who lived from 1912 to 1992 (a span of eighty years) would have experienced every form of government in the country's history. Those governments have included:

- **Feudalism:** Until 1912, major landowners dealt with the Turkish administration, which was then in power. The average citizen had no voice in government.
- **Monarchy:** A man called Ahmed Bey Zogu declared himself King Zog I of Albania in 1928 and ruled as dictator until 1939.
- **Fascism:** During World War II, from 1939 to 1945, Albania

Albanian children play with the giant letters of a Communist slogan thrown from the top of the party's headquarters during the anti-Communist riots of 1991.

was occupied and ruled by Fascist Italy and, briefly, by Nazi Germany.

- **Communism:** From 1946 to 1992, Albania experienced a Communist dictatorship. The government was headed by a former teacher and shopkeeper named Enver Hoxha.
- **Democracy:** In 1992, the first free elections brought hope that democracy would take hold in Albania.

A Democracy?

Is Albania now a democracy? The most accurate answer is that the country is headed in a democratic direction. At the moment, an elected president—Sali Berisha—presides over a

European-style government that includes a prime minister and a cabinet. The president and the prime minister run the country with the aid of cabinet members. The parliament has been freely elected since 1992.

The prime minister, who reports to the president, is in charge of the cabinet. Members include a deputy prime minister and minister of finance, a deputy prime minister and minister of construction and tourism, and a cabinet secretary. Besides those three positions there are ministers for agriculture and food; culture, youth, and sports; defense; education; energy and mineral resources; foreign affairs; health and environmental protection; industry, trade, and transport; interior and local government affairs; justice; and labor, social affairs, emigration, and affairs of former political prisoners. There is also a chairman of the science and technology committee and a chairman of state control. Each supervises a department of government workers.

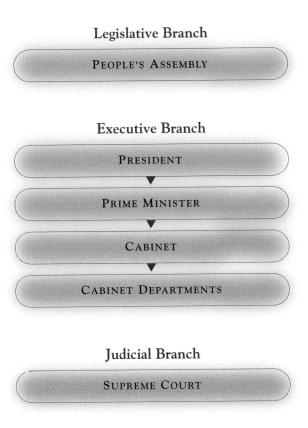

Legislative Branch

PEOPLE'S ASSEMBLY

Executive Branch

PRESIDENT

▼

PRIME MINISTER

▼

CABINET

▼

CABINET DEPARTMENTS

Judicial Branch

SUPREME COURT

Chart of Albania's national government

A Multiparty System

Ministers and government workers are members of several different political parties. Most belong to the Democratic Party. Former Communists call their party the Socialist Party of Albania. Other parties range from various socialist organiza-

A Historic Flag

Albania's flag has changed very little since it was first hoisted over Skenderbeg's battlefield in 1443. The black, two-headed eagle on a rectangle of red fluttered above the spot where the great hero decided to leave the Turks and fight for Albanian independence.

Down through the years, "Skenderbeg's flag" has remained the same, though the banner was not often raised while the country was under Turkish control. But, following World War I, the flag was a common sight. When Communists swept Albania after World War II, they added a red star (a traditional Communist symbol) above the two-headed eagle. The star disappeared after democracy gained a foothold in 1992.

tions to a Democratic Party of the Right. There are numerous independent (non-party) officeholders, and there is even a party called the Union for Human Rights, representing Albania's Greek minority.

A national legislature is made up of members representing all parts of the country. One hundred are elected directly by the people and forty are elected by proportional representation—that is, by the parties with the largest numbers of members.

The legal system was in limbo for a while because a new constitution, replacing the Communist constitution, was rejected by voters in 1994. With no constitution for guidance, police departments and court systems were only as good as their individual justices and law-enforcement administrators. But that recently changed.

For politicians everywhere, one of their main concerns is getting elected, then getting reelected. In events leading up to the March 1996 parliamentary election, the ruling Democratic Party was concerned that the Socialist Party of Albania—the former Communists—would regain control. They had reason to be fearful of a return to Communist dictatorship. Also, a number of Albanians have accused the Democrats of being corrupt and incompetent. However, a new law decrees that no former Communist can hold office until the year 2002. Former Communists and others say the law is illegal and undemocratic.

No party would have had an easy time running the country in the 1990s because Albania is making a painful switch from a rigidly controlled economy to a free-market economy.

Posters from the 1996 election

The change to a free-market economy means the end of government supports as well as Communist banners like the ones in this textile factory in Berat.

No longer will inefficient industries be propped up by the government. Businesses and industries will succeed or fail on their own. Many of the state's largest factories have already been purchased by private groups and individuals. In such an environment, bribery and other corrupt practices can—and do—take place.

Human Rights

The Democratic Party has also been accused of violating the human rights of its citizens. Of great concern was the recent firing of the chairman of the Supreme Court. A person in that high position was meant to be impartial and beyond the reach of the government. Another cause for concern is the govern-

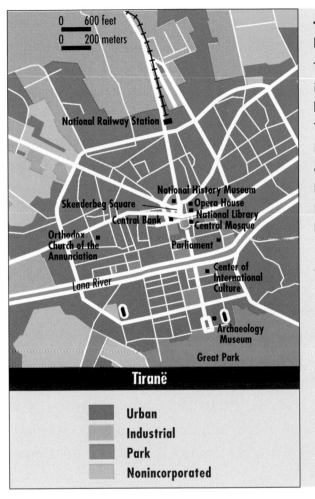

Tiranë

- Urban
- Industrial
- Park
- Nonincorporated

Map labels: National Railway Station, National History Museum, Skenderbeg Square, Opera House, National Library, Central Bank, Central Mosque, Orthodox Church of the Annunciation, Parliament, Lana River, Center of International Culture, Archaeology Museum, Great Park

0 600 feet
0 200 meters

Tiranë: Did You Know This?

The capital city of Tiranë is almost exactly halfway between Rome and Istanbul. The city was founded in 1614 by an Ottoman commander named Barkinzadah Suleiman Pasha. When Tiranë became the capital in 1920, it had only 12,000 residents. Today, it has about 300,000.

Tiranë lies at foot of the Daiti Mountains, about 200 feet (60 m) above sea level. During July, temperatures reach an average of 75°F (24°C), and during January, they reach 44°F (7°C). Tiranë averages 54 inches (137 cm) of rain per year.

ment's human-rights record, particularly charges involving Greek-speaking Albanians in the southeast part of the country.

Part of the problem is that Albania is not accustomed to an open democratic government. Public officials who for years were allowed to terrorize people now do not know how far they should go in enforcing the law. Government workers are equally unsure of their authority. They either order citizens around as before or simply let work pile up for fear of taking action. The government had no experienced people. Albania wasn't ready for democracy when it arrived.

The reviving nation now has ties with North America. Long before the U.S. government provided financial aid, people of Albanian descent in Boston, Cleveland, Detroit, New York, St. Louis, Toronto, and elsewhere sent money to relatives and worked for political, economic, social, and religious freedom. There is genuine pro-Western sentiment in the country.

Albania's Army

Under Communism in 1966, all military ranks disappeared. They were not restored until 1991. Fortunately, the Communist government never planned an attack, but they lived in constant fear that their country would be overrun. And because Albania under Communism lost a lot of friends, the enemy might have come from any direction. For more than forty years, ordinary citizens were trained as partisans— guerrilla soldiers. Every farm had its own small bunker and group of trainees. Today, only younger persons are taken into the armed forces—for two years in the navy and air force or one year in the army.

The Communists had good reason to fear combat: Albania's army was the worst equipped in Europe. Their tanks—aging Soviet machines—would have been all but helpless clanking around beneath modern airpower. Some

soldiers carried rifles left over from World War II. Missile technology was all but unknown and jet aircraft were outmoded. Today, the armed forces are being modernized under European and American supervision.

A young military-school student

Tensions between Albania and Yugoslavia have mounted in recent years. This is a border crossing between the two countries.

A united Europe and the disappearance of European Communism have reduced prospects of war. However, the situation in nearby Kosovo remains tense, as the Serbian minority has tried to repress the national aspirations of the large Albanian majority.

An Economy In Transition

During the first years after Communism, Albanians suffered a great deal. Food and clothing were scarce, and prices skyrocketed while wages fell. But by 1993, things began to change. In private hands, agriculture produced larger crops, while small businesses sprung up everywhere. Much of the money needed to buy seed, farm implements, and consumer goods came from the 500,000 Albanian emigrants employed in Germany, Greece, Italy, and other places. Prices in 1995 became much more stable.

Now, if an Albanian can afford them, all kinds of consumer goods are available. Japanese radios and television sets, French perfume, German cars, Italian clothing and furniture—these and other items are flowing into Albania as never before. Parents and children enjoy American breakfast cereal, African bananas, and canned Argentine beef for the first time. Unfortunately, these wonderful goods are entering Albania much faster than Albanian goods are being exported. That means the country is picking up debt because Albania's citizens want so many foreign products.

Since the move toward a free-market economy, more and more foreign goods have become available to the average Albanian.

Bills and Coins

Paper money in several denominations is common in Albania today, but coins are sometimes scarce. The highest paper denomination in circulation often seen is the 1,000-lek note. It shows the helmeted hero Skenderbeg on the front and a hillside fortress and the familiar two-headed eagle on the back. The paper is various shades of green. Smaller denominations are purple or blue or reddish-brown.

Fruit is one of Albania's leading export goods. This fruit-processing plant is in Peshkopi.

And there are other problems. Very few homes have central heating, so electric space heaters have sold by the thousands. This has caused brownouts and other malfunctions. The government realizes that its own people need more electrical power, but that means less electricity to sell to other countries—and even more debt for Albania. As of 1996, the value of imported goods was three times that of exports.

Plans are under way to replace small bills with coins. A 10-lek silver coin minted in 1992 shows Olympic boxers on one side and the two-headed eagle on the other. The words Shqipëria and Albania are imprinted into the coin, which weighs about 0.8 ounce (23 g).

What Does Albania Sell to the World?

Fruits and vegetables are among the leading items, including olives, figs, and oranges. Metallic ores, especially chrome and copper, scrap iron, iron and steel, crude oil, clothing, footwear,

Beautiful handmade carpets are another Albanian export item. Here, weavers work barefooted.

textiles, and manufactured goods such as rugs are in demand by Germany, Greece, Italy, and Macedonia, among other countries.

People and Property

Among the country's biggest problems at the moment is privatization—transferring houses, apartments, small plots of land, and other properties from government control to private

ownership. Many Albanians are waiting to be ordered out of a
home so that the new, private owner can move in. Albanians
generally marry young and have large families. These families
find themselves desperate for places to live, partly because the

Homelessness in Albania has hit young families hard.

elderly have been given preferential treatment where housing is concerned. A recent report indicated that an astonishing 75,000 people in Tiranë—one quarter of the total population—had no permanent home.

The two most valuable kinds of businesses going private are power-distribution companies and banks. The government is eager for private companies to make more electrical power, and they feel going private is the way to do it. Banks are being sold because,

What Albania Grows, Makes, and Mines	
Agriculture	
Wheat	470,000 metric tons
Corn	180,000 metric tons
Potatoes	100,000 metric tons
Manufacturing	
Cement	197,000 metric tons
Bricks	90 million
Phosphate fertilizer	22,000 metric tons
Mining	
Crude petroleum	585,000 metric tons
Coal	366,000 metric tons
Chromium	322,000 metric tons

with foreign banks coming in, they must prepare to compete. Officials hope more liberal banking and tax laws will solve some problems.

The privatization of banking in Albania is crucial for a successful transition to a free market.

High unemployment remains the biggest economic concern. With an unemployment rate estimated at 20 percent, 10 percent of all government spending goes toward supporting unemployed people and their families.

Another concern, one that is common in all developing countries, is the issue of child labor. Paid badly and sometimes abused, some 17,000 Albanian children under the age of fourteen are said to be fully employed, usually in agriculture on family farms.

Help from Abroad

The International Bank for Reconstruction and Development has given $4 million to boost small businesses. The European Union is rebuilding several potentially busy east-west roads. The Italians and the Swiss are giving Albania electric meters to stop the theft of power, which is common. The United States has pledged $46 million in aid, bringing a recent four-year total to $200 million. Other countries giving money, goods, or expertise include Germany, Greece, Japan, and Kuwait.

Phoning Home in Albania

The good news is that a German firm, working with the government, is installing a new fiberoptic telephone network. The bad news is that the telephone system now in place is overused and inefficient. Usually, long-distance calls must be placed through an operator. Almost all telephones belong to the government and businesses. There are only about 100,000 phones in all of Albania.

Child labor is the unfortunate result of a failing economy.

The People

Most of Albania's people are young. At the age of twenty-six, Albanians are usually married but not yet old enough to have teenage children. They are most likely to speak the Tosk dialect, follow the Muslim faith, and live in a rural area or a small village. They grow many of their own vegetables on a small plot of land acquired from the government, and live in a cramped apartment or small house without running water—and probably without indoor plumbing. Electricity is available in all but the most remote areas, however.

THESE YOUNG ALBANIAN ADULTS ARE LITERATE. THEY recently acquired a license to drive but have no car; most know how to use but do not own a telephone; and they keep up with local news, often by chatting with neighbors at the market.

Before the fall of Communism, Albanian citizens were often required to work maintaining local railroads.

They probably own a radio and a television set. Few such couples have a savings account, but they may hide small sums of cash, together with ancient coins and family heirlooms. The average couple has three children and may soon have more.

Until 1991, neither of these people has even been close to an airplane. They may have traveled by train once or twice, and they—and their parents—may have spent time building and maintaining railroads before the fall of Communism.

These people probably have only one or two changes of clothes. Their clothing is inexpensive, and was purchased locally. Each member of the family may have only one pair of shoes.

The husband is probably employed in agriculture, though with the move away from central farm ownership he could be out of work now, or underemployed. The wife takes care of the house, cooks the meals, and may add to the family's income by weaving rugs at home in her spare time. For this family, entertainment consists of an occasional wedding or festival, reading, and listening to their radio. They worship at a mosque on a somewhat regular basis. Their daily struggle to obtain life's necessities takes up much of their time.

Without easy access to drinking water, some Albanians are forced to collect it from natural springs, which can be a time-consuming chore.

Language

Because no other modern language is quite like Albanian, it is difficult to learn. The first thing a foreigner may notice is that there are thirty-six letters in the Albanian alphabet. Taking a closer look, many of these letters seem to be repeated.

For example, the letter c is reproduced twice, once as an ordinary letter c and once as a c with a tiny hook dangling from it—ç. To complicate matters, the ordinary c is pronounced as English speakers would pronounce *ts*, while the c with the little hook is pronounced as we would pronounce *ch*.

Double letters in the language are a part of the alphabet. They include dh, pronounced *th*; gj, pronounced *du*; ll, pronounced *l*; nj, pronounced *n*; rr, pronounced like a rolling r—*rrrrr*; sh and *th*, pronounced as they appear; xh pronounced *j*; and zh, pronounced *su*.

Any European listening to an Albanian speaker might hear an occasional word that sounds familiar because a number of words and phrases have been borrowed from Italian, Greek, and other languages. But scholars believe the vast majority of Albanian words come from the Illyrian. To complicate matters, many words are spoken with a lisp.

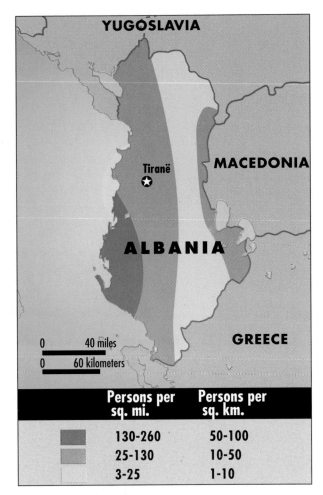

Persons per sq. mi.	Persons per sq. km.
130-260	50-100
25-130	10-50
3-25	1-10

Map of the population distribution in Albania

Who Lives in Albania?

Albanians	95%
Greeks	3%
Other*	2%

* Macedonians, Montenegrins, Serbs, Croats, Romanies (formerly known as Gypsies), Bulgarians, and Vlachs

By law, Albanians must attend school until the age of fifteen. This means they receive eight years of formal education. Only in the most remote mountains are children taken out of school, usually to do farmwork. Most schools are public,

Like most public services in Albania, education has limited resources.

Opposite: Students at the University of Tiranë, the country's first university

though since the fall of Communism a number of church-related schools have sprung up. The ministry of education sets a standard course for all grade levels.

Albania has several universities, and professors there are free to substitute whatever books they see fit, so long as general guidelines set by the government are followed. All courses are taught in the Albanian language except at the University of Gjirokastër, which offers classes in the Greek language and

Common Albanian Words and Phrases

hello	**tungjatjeta** (tun-doo-a-YEA-tuh)
good-bye	**mirupafshim** (mear-up-AHF-shum)
please	**lutemi** (loo-TEE-me)
thanks	**faleminderit** (fahl-uh-mun-DAIR-ut)
yes	**po**
no	**jo**
one	**nje** (nyay)
two	**dy** (die)
three	**tre** (tray)
four	**katcr** (cottcr)
five	**pese** (pace)

Five Largest Cities in Albania	
Tiranë	300,200
Durrës	85,400
Elbasan	83,300
Shkodër	81,900
Vlorë	73,800

Waiting for the bus

on Greek culture. Because of the nation's limited transportation, several schools also offer correspondence courses.

Getting Around

Enver Hoxha believed his country needed railroads so he saw to it that more than 400 miles (645 km) of track were laid. Most trains arrive in and leave Tiranë on a daily basis. The diesel engines and Italian-made passenger coaches visit Durrës and Elbasan as well as Shkodër, Vlorë, and towns between.

Riding a train can be comfortable, but driving in Albania can be an ordeal. Roads are narrow and poorly maintained, drivers are inexperienced, and delays can be caused by rock

slides, floods, police roadblocks, and more. Some rural areas can be reached only by four-wheel-drive vehicles. Buses are generally old and crowded, and frequently break down. Taxis travel between cities and can be shared.

Albania has a dozen airports, only one of which handles major commercial traffic. Two others are closed and most of the rest have been used by the military. Tiranë's commercial runways are being lengthened. There are no commercial flights between Albanian cities at present.

Albanians Abroad

As much as they love their country, Albanians have never hesitated to leave—to find work or to escape a repressive government. Today, more than 5 million people of Albanian heritage live outside the country, compared to 3.5 million in Albania. For example, the United States is now home to about 350,000 Albanian-Americans who continue to show concern for the Land of the Eagle. The largest group, about 150,000, is in the greater New York City area. They are Eastern Orthodox, Muslim, and Roman Catholic.

Boston has an Albanian community centered around the Albanian Orthodox Archdiocese in America, while Worcester, Massachusetts, 48 miles (77 km) west of Boston, is home to Albanians who are mostly Eastern Orthodox. Detroit has a number of Albanian Muslims and Roman Catholics, and people of Albanian descent also live in Chicago, Cleveland, Philadelphia, as well as California and Florida. Many of these people left Communist Albania for religious freedom.

Albanian-Americans are indistinguishable from the millions of other Americans of European descent, but there is one important difference. Many of them send money, food, clothing, and other essentials to relatives in Albania. Until

the fall of Communism, only a few people with relatives in Albania were allowed to enter the country.

A small number group of Albanians have crossed the Adriatic Sea to live in Italy. The ancestors of these people, who were either Eastern Orthodox or Roman Catholic, fled Albania when the Turks moved in. They settled in remote parts of southern Italy and in Sicily in villages about 1,500 feet (460 m) above sea level. Small Albanian-speaking villages are found to this day, but modern communications will probably have them speaking Italian in a generation or two.

Other large and permanent settlements of Albanians can be found in Macedonia and parts of Yugoslavia. Along with Greece, which has a number of Muslim Albanians known as Chams, these countries share a border with Albania.

In the past, Albanians have been eager for opportunities abroad. In 1990, for example, thousands of refugees sailed by boat to the Italian port of Brindisi.

Three Faiths, One God

Religion has played an important part in the lives of Albanians since before Christianity swept westward along the Mediterranean shores some 2,000 years ago. One key date in Albania's religious history is A.D. 70, when Caesarus, a disciple of Jesus Christ, became the first bishop of the city of Durrës.

Another important date is 1054, the year the Christian Church broke into two: Roman Catholic and Orthodox. And in 1478, Turkey overran parts of Albania and brought the Islamic religion with them.

Also critical was the year 1945, when anti-religious Communists decreed what people should believe, and 1990, when they gave up that control. Since 1990, Albanians have been able to worship in churches and mosques and make public displays of their faith.

Today's foreign clergy and missionaries are free to perform religious activities. At present, Sunni Muslim clergy are trained in Egypt, while the Albanian Orthodox Church has been training new priests in Albania since 1994. Roman Catholic seminaries are opening in northern Albania. Orthodox priests from Greece serve Greek-speaking congregations in southern Albania.

Although all three major faiths believe in the same god, they worship in very different ways.

Members of Albania's Eastern Orthodox Church celebrate Easter in Tiranë.

Religions of Albania

Muslim	60%
Orthodox	25%
Roman Catholic	15%

Three Faiths, One God **95**

A Muslim studies the Koran inside Tiranë's Central Mosque.

This religion, with followers around the globe, began in Saudi Arabia in the 600s with the prophet Muhammad. Muhammad felt himself called to be God's prophet. His teachings are recorded in a book called the Koran, which is as important to a Muslim as the Bible is to a Christian.

A Muslim's duties are listed in the five Pillars of Faith. First, a person must recite the following: "There is no God but Allah, and Muhammad is his prophet." Second, a Muslim must pray five times daily at specific hours, preferably in a mosque. Third, Muslims must be willing to give alms to the poor. Fourth, followers of Islam must not eat or drink from sunrise to sunset during the holy month of Ramadan, the ninth month in the Muslim calendar. Fifth, a Muslim must make a pilgrimage to Mecca, Saudi Arabia, at least once.

Often, visitors are aware they are in a Muslim country by the dramatic sound of the local muezzin calling his people to prayer. That sound was not heard in Albania for nearly half a century during Communist rule, but now it echoes at all the proper times. As there is a shortage of mosques, some Albanian Muslims assemble at a central gathering place to pray.

This is a traditional Albanian mosque, complete with minaret, in Berat. Albania is the only European country in which Islam is the predominate religion.

Mother Teresa—A Famous Albanian

Mother Teresa was born Agnes Gonxha Bojaxhiu in Skopje in 1910, the daughter of an Albanian grocer. Always small and somewhat fragile in appearance, she was eighteen when she sailed to Ireland to join the Institute of the Blessed Virgin Mary as a nun. Because of dire needs in other parts of the world, Teresa found herself sailing to India only six weeks later.

She was assigned initially to teach in a Roman Catholic mission. But after working in the classroom and spending her spare time as the school principal, she asked in 1948 to serve the poor people of Calcutta. These people live and die on the busy streets of a dirty city so thick with population that it often ceases to function.

Mother Teresa learned enough about medicine to move into the worst slums and begin treating street people with all sorts of illnesses. A weaker person would have been overwhelmed by the number of blind, sick, and poverty-stricken human beings living in filth. But the tiny nun became a citizen of India, nursing the poor while she trained Indian nuns in her Calcutta clinic.

The religious order she began—the Missionaries of Charity—now has thousands of sisters and brothers around the world, most in India. They shelter thousands of orphans, teach thousands more in schools, care for hundreds of thousands of people in free medical clinics, and aid lepers who are so deformed with their disease that no one else will go near them.

Pope Pius XII learned of her good works in 1950 and named Teresa's order a pon-tifical congregation—answerable only to the pope himself. She opened more and more clinics and set aside special places where the homeless could die with dignity. Her good works have inspired many religious and nonreligious people to give money or work in her clinics.

Those who meet Mother Teresa are surprised by her forceful personality. Without a touch of sentimentality, she is an utter realist—aware of how much good she has done and aware that there is much more to do. She has visited strife-torn Northern Ireland, where she talked with British soldiers and joined several groups to pray for peace.

After decades of service, through world wars, the achieving of independence by India, in monsoon rains and blistering heat, Mother Teresa was awarded the Nobel Peace Prize in 1979. She is, said a recent pope, "an example and symbol of the discovery . . . that man is our brother." Today, despite failing health, she is among the most widely known and greatly admired people of the twentieth century.

Mosques are as distinctive as churches. Every mosque has a minaret, a thin tower from which the muezzin traditionally calls the faithful to prayer. Today, in larger towns, the call may be made with a Japanese-crafted boom box or a German-made tape player and speakers. Since Islam prohibits art that represents living things, don't look for rich paintings inside a mosque. Instead, endless patterns and shapes cover everything, including a central prayer room.

Men and women use separate doors to enter a mosque. Once inside, they wash their hands, arms, and faces in a large, shallow pool of water, and enter separate prayer rooms, leaving their shoes in a courtyard. The *imam* or priest may give a brief sermon after the people bow in prayer. Muslims usually assemble in orderly rows of worshipers.

In Albania, many people follow a version of Islam not fully in keeping with the more strict methods of worship in the Middle East. Called Bektashism, this version of Islam was founded in Asia Minor in the 1200s and includes elements of ancient pagan religions and Christianity.

Many Bektashis drink alcohol, which is forbidden in the more fundamental branches of Islam. Calls to prayer are irregular or nonexistent, women do not wear veils (except during marriage ceremonies), worshipers are baptized and practice regular confession, and God is seen as a part of nature rather than a supreme being with whom a believer is in contact. Turks tried to stamp out Bektashism in Albania and Communists tried to stamp out all forms of Islam in Albania. Both failed utterly.

The Christian Churches—Divided

The Eastern Orthodox Church, known officially as the Orthodox Catholic Church, and the Roman Catholic Church were one church until 1054. At that time, they separated over a religious disagreement. Christians believe in God and his son, Jesus Christ. According to the New Testament of the Bible, Christ died on the cross to save us all, opening the way for humans to enter heaven.

This Albanian Orthodox church dates back to the 1300s.

Eastern Orthodoxy was headquartered in Constantinople, the capital of the Byzantine Empire. But the city was plundered in 1204 and in 1452 by the Turks, and the patriarchs, or leaders, of the Orthodox Church were under the control of Turkish rulers for several centuries. The church survived by spreading into Eastern Europe, particularly Russia. Albanian followers of the Orthodox religion practiced their faith behind closed doors.

Roman Catholic and Eastern Orthodox Albanians fled to Italy in large numbers when the Turks took over. Italy was nearby and, equally important, Rome was the headquarters of the Catholic faith. Catholics in Albania, like all religious people under Communism, kept their beliefs to themselves. Priests who attempted to conduct services or teach in parochial schools were shot or imprisoned.

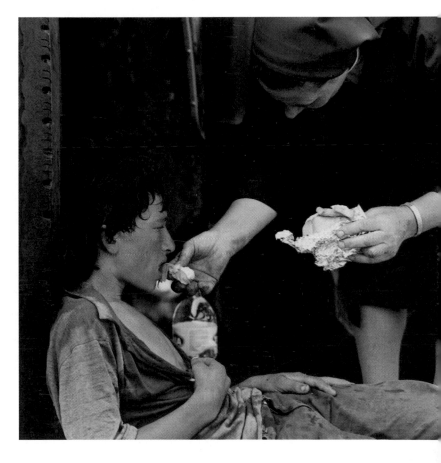

A Catholic nun helps a needy Albanian youth.

A visitor can tell the Christian churches apart with a little practice. Orthodox priests are allowed to marry, they often wear more elaborate clothing than their Roman Catholic counterparts, and there are visible differences in the services. Orthodox priests conduct much of the Mass facing the altar, with their backs to worshipers. Catholic priests face the parishioners.

Since World War II, prosperous Albanians in other parts of the world have funneled food, clothing, and other essentials into their homeland through churches. Americans have been especially generous, giving to family and strangers alike to help the people survive the years of hardship. Followers of all three faiths have been equally giving.

Religion Today

Albania is the only country lying entirely within the European continent where most of the people follow Islam. Today, despite several decades of atheistic Communist rule, 60 percent of the people call themselves either Bektashi or Sunni Muslims. More than 25 percent are Orthodox Christians, while about 15 percent are Roman Catholic.

Such a mix, combined with a few people of Bulgarian, Greek, or Romany (formerly known as Gypsy) descent, might seem to make Albania potentially explosive, like the former Yugoslavia. However, because of their shared struggle for independence, the Albanian people have developed religious tolerance.

You can admit to being anything but an atheist in today's Albania, says an expert on the country. People who claim to be atheists are thought to be Communists and therefore supporters of the disgraced Hoxha and Alia regimes. Like

everything else in Albania, religion is in a state of change. Now that the people may worship as they choose, religion has become less important to those who are more interested in material things.

A number of Christian missionaries, primarily from the United States and Great Britain, have gone to Albania to introduce or convert people to Protestantism. Some Albanians resent these visitors while others have accepted the missionaries. Meanwhile, historic churches and mosques are being rebuilt for worshipers and for tourists.

Religious tolerance is a major feature of Albanian society. This was especially true in World War II, when Albanian Jews were aided in escaping Nazi persecution. Albanians today often point out that their country, war-torn as it was, did not round up Jews for the Nazi concentration camps.

Albanians take part in the first freely celebrated Christmas mass in the town of Shkodër on December 25, 1990. Until 1990, the government outlawed religious services.

A Living Museum

E vidence of Albania's history is not confined to museums. It is all around a visitor to the small country. Ruins of the ancient Greeks and Romans, the Ottoman Turks, the German Nazis, and the Communists are everywhere. A brief stop in some important cities and towns will bring history and culture alive.

The National History Museum's mural looms over Skenderbeg Square in Tiranë, recalling former Communist days.

THE MOST COMMON WAY TO enter Albania these days is aboard a regularly scheduled jet plane. Austrian, Bulgarian, Czech, Dutch, German, Greek, Italian, and Swiss aircraft land regularly at Tiranë's Rinas Airport, some 14 miles (23 km) from the capital city. Tiranë sits on a plain in the middle of the country, so there is seldom any snow, but a glance to the east reveals snow-covered peaks much of the year. The road into the city of 300,000 is a narrow strip of pocked asphalt that is being expanded.

Tiranë—The Capital City

Until about 1995 there was little vehicle traffic—and by European or North American standards, there still isn't. It's fairly easy to drive into Skenderbeg Square, the center of Tiranë. Except for trucks, cars, and some construction, you don't hear the usual big-city noise. One visitor noted a few years ago that the sound he heard most often each morning was birds singing. On the square are the National History Museum, the Soviet-built Palace of Culture that is being turned into a library, the Geographical Institute, the Central

Bank, a hotel, and government buildings. The square is several blocks wide.

Tiranë is the home of the country's university, all central government offices, and the most likely place to find once-scarce consumer goods. Today, Albanians can buy cheeseburgers, cassette recordings, fresh fruit out of season, or fashionable Italian shoes or clothing—if they have the money. Small stores are opening all the time and the same store may sell clothing, medicine, cosmetics, junk food, and motor scooters.

Other important sites in Tiranë, which is by far the country's largest city, include the International Trade Center, the Archaeology Museum, the Clock Tower, the Central Mosque, and the Orthodox Church of the Annunciation. There are many new travel agencies, shops, restaurants, bars, and nonalcoholic refreshment stands. Tiranë stands on the site of a fortress built in 500 b.c., but it looks toward the twenty-first century.

So far, only a few high-rise hotels block the views of church spires, mosques, or mountains. The tallest building, a fifteen-story hotel structure, is nowhere near as lofty as the castles on the hills around the city. According to the historians, Tiranë was founded in 1614 when a Turkish sultan built a mosque and several baths here.

Opposite: **People taking an evening stroll through Tiranë's city center**

Durrës—An Ancient Port City

Albania's second largest city is only a fraction the size of Tiranë and is convenient to the capital. Durrës is a port city about 30 miles (48 km) due west. It became well known in the early 1990s as the place where young Albanian men desperate to leave the country jumped aboard overcrowded, dangerous old scows, hoping to sail to the port of Bari in

The port of Durrës

Italy. Today, as more and more goods flow into the country, it is a bustling seaport of about 85,000 residents.

Founded by ancient Greeks and used extensively by the Romans, Durrës marked the start of a great Roman road that wound eastward across the peninsula to Constantinople. Like Tiranë, Durrës was built atop ruins of great significance. Consequently, special permits are

required before any digging associated with construction can take place. At one time or another, Venetians, Turks, Italians, and Germans controlled the city and the port.

A huge mosque stands in the center of town, along with an Orthodox chapel, a Roman amphitheater, and Roman baths. King Zog had a palace built for himself here that looks out over the sea toward Italy. Nowadays, television antennas are pointed westward across the Strait of Otranto in an effort to pick up Italian entertainment. The ancient buildings look strange covered with antennas, but modern communications played an important role in letting Communist Albania know of European progress.

The roof tiles here glow especially red in the oceanside sun, making a lovely contrast with the cream-colored build-

These pillars are just one example of Roman architecture in Durrës.

Durrës's dramatic red-tiled roofs

ings and the wide, sandy beach. Visitors enjoy the puppet theater and the parks and gardens dotted with rosebushes, as well as the many historic ruins and monuments.

A cloud of pollution hangs over the industrial center of Elbasan.

Elbasan—An Industrial Center

Albania's third-largest city, Elbasan, is about the same size as Durrës and lies approximately the same distance from Tiranë, but to the south. Though the city is set amid groves of olive and orange trees, it's not the heavenly place one might imagine. Heavy industry, with few pollution controls, shrouds the valleys in coal smoke. The only consolation is that the big, inefficient steel mill here is no longer in operation.

Illyrians founded Elbasan, which gives you an idea of its great age. The city was once surrounded by a stone wall, and some of that centuries-old fortification still stands today. The mosques and churches here are intricately decorated, the former with wonderful abstract designs, the latter with vivid biblical frescoes. The museum in Elbasan has a wonderful display of historic Albanian clothing, plus a number of crafts.

From Shkodër to Krujë

Several smaller cities and towns notable for their history include Shkodër, Gjirokastër, Berat, Vlorë, and Krujë.

Shkodër was built on the east end of Lake Shkodër. The city stands in the northern mountains near Montenegro. The landscape is dominated by majestic Rozafat Castle. Other scenic areas include the Turkish baths, the lakeshore, and the ancient houses along the many narrow streets surrounded by tall stone walls. This city, which has always been considered Albania's cultural center, has a university, a library with more than 350,000 books, and many historic monuments. It is also the center of Roman Catholicism in Albania.

The northern city of Shkodër

Products made in Shkodër include wire and cables, leather goods, wood products, and tobacco. At one time, this city had the biggest Turkish-style market in the Balkan Peninsula. A rail line from Shkodër links Albania with the rest of Europe.

Gjirokastër lies at the opposite end of the country, only about 20 miles (32 km) from Greece. Gjirokastër is the birthplace of both Communist dictator Enver Hoxha and Ismail Kadare, the country's most widely known author. A fortress built here by the Illyrians in the 500s is still in good condition. This is a handsome and well-preserved town, with large houses on picturesque cobblestone streets. The houses are made of stucco and often have spacious lobbies and intricate, wood-carved interiors.

The fortress and old town of Gjirokastër

Albanians consider Gjirokastër a "museum town." One museum here displays a small airplane said to be a U.S. spy plane shot down in 1957. The National Folk Festival is held each year in this city built on the piney hills. Food and tobacco are processed here.

The town of Berat overlooks Osum River.

A Roman basilica at Butrint

Berat, about halfway between Gjirokastër and Tiranë, is Albania's other "museum town." Located above a gorge, this city is painted almost entirely in white and looks like an improbable movie set. The fortress here is well preserved, even though it is almost 2,400 years old. The oldest mosque in Albania is here too, along with half a dozen historic churches. The brilliant religious icons and fresco paintings in these buildings are priceless treasures.

Vlorë is the nation's second-largest port after Durrës. Albania's navy is based here. Ancient ruins can be found all around the southwest coast, and the coastal road south from Vlorë takes visitors to several diggings and then to Butrint. Butrint is a village virtually unchanged since the time of the Romans. The only problem is how to display its treasures without having them carried off, or overrun, by enthusiastic tourists.

Vlorë has a clock tower, a market, and a sixteenth-century mosque. It has been known since early Roman times for its wine, olives, and salt. The many ugly apartment buildings built here during the Communist era are overshadowed today by spacious tourist hotels set along a lovely beach.

Whoever founded Krujë realized that this city's mountain air stayed cool in the summer. Visitors enjoy the beautiful and well-preserved Turkish baths, and the museum devoted to Skenderbeg that is set inside a stately castle. Olive trees and lime kilns dot the countryside.

The Skenderbeg Museum in Krujë

A colorful Durrës dusk

Rural Albania—Scenes of Color

More than half of the Albanian people live in tiny villages or in the country. They tend their gardens and fields and raise livestock. At one time of the day or other, it may seem to the traveler that they are all trying to use the roads—which are narrow, winding, without guardrails, and in growing need of repair. Tractors, buses, flocks of sheep, trucks, bicyclists, farm wagons, and pedestrians seem to be around every bend, so driving quickly is out of the question.

On the other hand, the views are sensational, particularly on a clear day, looking from a high mountain out to sea. And despite the great age of many farm buildings, rural life is often picturesque. Imagine brilliant red peppers strung against a whitewashed wall for drying. Harvests of grapes, grains, and vegetables are equally colorful.

Enjoying Salt Water and Fresh Water

Hundreds of yachts bob at anchor around the coastal city of Butrint, opposite the Greek isle of Corfu. Warm the year round, this little corner of Albania is crowded with vacationers in winter and the entire coastline is sure to become even more popular as tourist accommodations increase. In contrast, highland lakes are difficult to reach and seldom visited by tourists.

In addition to the three large lakes shared with Montenegro, Macedonia, and Greece are the six Lurë Lakes. In a national park about 50 miles (80 km) northwest of Tiranë, these lakes are free of signs of civilization except for picnic grounds and an occasional fisher. They are difficult to reach in good weather and entirely off limits in bad.

Appreciating the Arts

The Albanians have a deep appreciation of culture, be it an ancient Greek fresco or a modern Italian aria. The fresco is carefully preserved, while the music is enjoyed on thousands of radios.

A number of literary and other kinds of publications sprouted when Communism fell, mainly in the nation's capital. Dance has always been a popular form of entertainment for young people, while men's choirs sing rousing or emotional folk songs and other tunes.

Radio provides the latest news and music in Albania. Here employees of Radio Tiranë sort through mail.

Teenagers sip coffee and watch Italian soccer on TV.

Visual arts, long considered subversive or useless by the Communists, are just now reawakening.

The present government encourages preservation of Albanian folk traditions and there are some 4,300 cultural institutions throughout the country. The national library, the state choir, the state opera, and the national ballet in Tiranë are supported with government funds.

Watching and Playing Sports

Soccer is the most popular sport in Albania, and the national team has competed in world championships for several years. Basketball, which is growing in popularity, and soccer are sometimes shown on television. Other sports on TV are auto, bicycle, and motorcycle racing, though most such events take place elsewhere in Europe.

People in Albania are active in a variety of sports. In school, volleyball and wrestling are the most popular sports. Swimming is also popular, and along the coast, the swimming season runs from May through September. Though Albania's ski hills are not well developed, the countryside is mountainous. Well-equipped climbers in Albania take on challenging peaks and brave the altitude. Bicycling also is gaining popularity, despite the crude roads and the steep hills.

Ismail Kadare: Albanian Author

Ismail Kadare is Albania's greatest living writer. Like Mother Teresa, his name has been associated with the Nobel Prize. Literary experts say he is overdue for the honor.

Born in 1936, he is from Gjirokastër, the same city as Enver Hoxha. Not much is known about his boyhood years, but he graduated from Tiranë University and studied in Moscow on a scholarship. Kadare's education was cut short in 1961 when Albania severed relations with the Soviet Union.

Returning to Albania, the thin young man with glasses quickly produced a novel, *The General of the Dead Army*, which was published in 1963. It tells the story of an retired Italian general who must identify the bodies of his soldiers who died in Albania during World War II.

The novel was seen by the authorities as patriotic and anti-Italian. It could be read as a comparison of corrupt Western values to the wholesome Albanian way of life. Though some Albanians saw it as a satire against militarism, it was warmly received by government officials.

Kadare's other books include a series of short stories, *The Southern City* (1964), *The Wedding* (1968), and *Chronicle in Stone* (1971). He was elected to the People's Assembly, Albania's national legislature, in the early 1970s. As Albania became the last holdout for hard-line Communism, the author's books contained more magic and fantastic themes.

Outside Albania, Kadare's reputation grew and his work was published in a dozen languages. However, during the 1970s, Kadare fell out of favor with his own government because he composed a poem that made fun of people in power. The powerful got their revenge, forcing him to live in a remote village and preventing him from publishing anything for three years.

By the early 1980s, the writer's career took an even stranger twist. Enver Hoxha, the aging dictator, began to write and to compete with Kadare. In Kadare's *The Palace of Dreams* (1981), he courageously wrote about an evil government that practiced mind control on its citizens. Hoxha permitted the book to be published, then had it banned shortly afterward. Perhaps the leader felt his autobiography, *The Wily Albanian*, was better reading.

In the 1980s, Kadare grew bolder with each book. He made fun of Albanian leaders and their friends, he complained of censorship, and he favorably reviewed anti-government books. The tottering Communist government asked for his opinion of reforms in 1990—and then disregarded it. He was threatened by the secret police. In October 1990, Kadare fled to Paris.

The author's defection stunned Albanians. It was as if Mark Twain had decided at the height of his career to leave the United States. Kadare's sudden departure sped up the reform that resulted in a non-Communist government for his country. At the moment, he, his wife, and his two daughters share a Paris apartment where he continues to write. The author, who now visits Albania frequently, wrote a popular book called *Pyramid* in 1996.

Daily Life

Roosters greet the sunrise in many parts of Albania. You hear their call everywhere in the countryside and on the outskirts of most cities. Another similarity between rural and urban life is that people in both places are likely to live in planned communities. These are concrete apartment buildings, where several families share kitchens and toilets. Such residences can even be found on large farms that were collective farms in the days of Communism.

This steelworker from Elbasan, like many Albanians, worries about job security.

Because there are so many young people in Albania, the cry of a baby is heard in many apartments. Despite the fact that young men leave the country to find work, so many babies are born that Albania's population is growing four to five times faster than those of other European countries. One-third of the people are under fifteen, so city and village streets are crowded with schoolchildren.

Country people rise early to work the land, tend their animals, and do farm chores. City and village dwellers get up a bit later. The father of a family may work in a store or factory, while the mother might sit at a loom, weaving rugs. So-called oriental rugs are in great demand in other countries. Their export has been a steady source of foreign money since 1990.

Limited Opportunities

Unemployment continues to be a problem, however. Large numbers of adults gather daily in coffeehouses. Many were employed in local factories that shut down because they were antiquated, or because they produced items that didn't sell.

Daily Life **119**

In 1997, many Albanians lost their life savings in various get-rich-quick schemes.

These people hope for the start-up of new business and industry. Major European manufacturers like Mercedes-Benz are now setting up sales and repair facilities across Albania. People who live near these planned dealerships hope to be hired.

Albanians sometimes operate with "mattress money"—money hidden away, little by little, during the Communist years, when there was nothing worth buying. Because the government cannot fully support the unemployed, families live on the money they saved or sell family heirlooms and antiques. The painful transition to a modern European nation can be seen in other instances:

- Early in 1997, Albanians took to the streets in large numbers all across the country. One citizen in seven had been the victim of various get-rich-quick schemes. The protesters believed that the government should repay those who lost their money because it had allowed the schemes to take place. Tiranë was the scene of many arrests as police waded into the crowd swinging batons at the demonstrators. At least a few of them may have been members of a political party opposed to the government.

- In contrast to the Communist years, foreigners are often seen in Tiranë and other major cities today. Many are European businesspeople, perhaps planning to locate a factory here, where wages are the lowest on the continent. To accommodate these visitors, several hotels have sprouted in and around the capital, providing jobs for local residents. The downside is that some foreigners have been victims of pickpockets and other thieves. Another problem is that Albanians often sell priceless heirlooms and artifacts to well-to-do foreigners for a fraction of their real worth.

- Most Albanian adults have received some religious training, even if it was behind closed doors many years ago. So there is some resentment when missionaries from Europe, the Middle East, and North America arrive in the country and treat the people as if they were heathens. Religions that are foreign to the locals, such as Mormonism, are also trying to gain followers, while familiar religions such as Islam are sometimes suspect—especially if representatives are militants from countries such as Iran or Libya.

> **Holidays in Albania**
> New Year's Day (January 1)
> Id al-Fitr (Little Bayram, the breaking of the fast)
> International Women's Day
> Roman Catholic Easter
> Eastern Orthodox Easter
> Id al-Adha (Great Bayram, the feast of the sacrifice)
> Labor Day (May 1)
> Independence and Liberation Day (November 28)
> Christmas (December 25)

Despite the rise in unemployment and crime, Albanians continue to welcome strangers. The average family spends their time watching television if they have one, listening to the radio, or playing chess or soccer. Most Albanians enjoy folk dancing at weddings and other celebrations. For Albanians, retaining their rich heritage as they modernize their country is just one more challenge.

Open-air markets in Albania offer a variety of fresh vegetables in season.

Shopping

Even though Albania is primarily a Muslim country, many shops close on Sunday. On other days of the week, they are generally open from 9 A.M. to noon and from 4 to 9 P.M. City-dwelling Albanians usually get off work around 4 P.M. and, with friends and family, go to popular downtown areas to walk around, enjoy a drink, or just chat. Handicrafts of all kinds are sold on the streets in both cities and villages.

The only holiday exclusive to Albania is Independence Day on November 28. Also observed are New Year's Day, Easter, Labor Day, Muslim Bayram, and Christmas. Ramadan, the holy month on the Islamic lunar calendar, means reduced activities in most cities where the majority of the population are Muslims.

Mediterranean Eating

Few Albanians are overweight. A major reasons for this is their Mediterranean-style diet. People who live around the shores of the Mediterranean Sea, from Spain eastward to Israel and from Israel westward through northern Africa, may be the world's healthiest diners. Their diets have changed very little over the centuries.

The main meal of the day is served about 1 P.M. It consists of small servings of meat such as beef, pork, lamb, chicken, or fish and rice, spaghetti, or white, brown, or corn bread, and vegetables. Vegetables on an Albanian table may include

A young entrepreneur sells sandwiches wrapped in scrap paper.

tomatoes, cucumbers, lettuce, cabbage, potatoes, beets, spinach, leeks and onions, eggplant, okra, peppers, carrots, and olives. The most frequently served side dishes are *pilaf* (a rice-and-cheese dish), fried potatoes, and cottage cheese. Thick yogurt mixed with garlic is served at many meals as a dressing.

A Coca-Cola bottling plant near the airport in Tiranë now supplies Albania with that popular soft drink. Other drinks include red and white wine, bottled water, and thimble-sized servings of strong coffee.

Desserts are not always included, but a pielike pastry called byrek may be offered, containing cheese, meat, leeks, pumpkin, or a combination of ingredients. Many meals end with oranges, apples, nuts, or berries.

Because they eat meat sparingly, consume many carbohydrates, and cook with olive oil, Albanians have less heart and artery disease than other Europeans. The evening meal, served about 8 P.M., is a smaller version of the mid-day meal, while breakfast may typically feature bread with honey or jam, milk or yogurt, and coffee or flavorful, yellowish Albanian tea.

Older Albanians

Albanians have good health care. Consequently, they live almost as long as other Europeans. The life expectancy at birth for men is about seventy; for women, about seventy-six. Grandparents sometimes live with their adult children, helping out as cooks, baby-sitters, shepherds, and general fixer-uppers. They are provided with government pensions, though their monthly support may be slow in coming because

Some Albanians carry on
with traditional ways.

the government is heavily in debt. Divorce among older people is virtually unknown but is expected to increase among younger people as European lifestyles become more common.

Meanwhile, grandparents occupy themselves with sewing, hanging colorful peppers out to dry at a farmstead, wearing their World War II medals during holiday parades, cooking tasty recipes from memory, or taking a grandchild into the mountains for an afternoon of fishing or hunting. Their children and grandchildren may have adopted the tennis shoes and jeans seen everywhere today, but these retirees continue to wear very plain and practical clothing.

The Future

Their adult children, despite the competition for jobs and the perpetual shortage of money, are hopeful. They see a better life for themselves and a bright future for their children. Albanians realize that, because of their rich cultural treasures and low standard of living, Europe is knocking at the door and wants to be invited in. And the traditionally generous Albanians are prepared to do whatever it takes to make their guests feel welcome.

Timeline

Albanian History

Illyrian civilization established in the Balkans.	2000–1000 B.C.
Greeks found colonies in what is now Albania.	800–500 B.C.
Philip of Macedonia conquers the Illyrians.	359 B.C.
Albanians come under Roman rule.	165 B.C.
Christianity reaches Albania.	1st century A.D.
Roman Empire splits, leaving Albania part of the Byzantine Empire.	A.D. 395
Goths, Huns, Lombards, Serbs, Croats, and Bulgars sweep across the Balkan Peninsula.	300s–600s
Ottoman Turks invade Albania.	1388
Skenderbeg and his army repulse Turkish forces. Skenderbeg dies in 1468.	1444–1468
Turks take control of Albania, making it part of the Ottoman Empire.	1478

World History

c. 2500 B.C.	Egyptians build the Pyramids and Sphinx in Giza.
563 B.C.	Buddha is born in India.
A.D. 313	The Roman emperor Constantine recognizes Christianity.
610	The prophet Muhammad begins preaching a new religion called Islam.
1054	The Eastern (Orthodox) and Western (Roman) Churches break apart.
1066	William the Conqueror defeats the English in the Battle of Hastings.
1095	Pope Urban II proclaims the First Crusade.
1215	King John seals the Magna Carta.
1300s	The Renaissance begins in Italy.
1347	The Black Death sweeps through Europe.
1453	Ottoman Turks capture Constantinople, conquering the Byzantine Empire.
1492	Columbus arrives in North America.
1500s	The Reformation leads to the birth of Protestantism.

Albanian History

Two-thirds of Albanians convert to Islam.	1600s–1700s
Ali Pasha assassinated by Ottomans for supporting Albanian Independence.	1822
Albania gains its independence.	1912
Ahmed Bey Zogu seizes power, beginning a fifteen-year reign.	1924
Italy invades Albania in April.	1939
Albania becomes a Communist nation.	1944
Albania breaks off relations with the Soviet Union.	1960
China cuts off aid to Albania.	1978
Enver Hoxha dies.	1985
Free elections are held after student protests; Communists win.	1991
Communists ousted in elections.	1992
Sali Berisha reelected. The country is threatened with anarchy.	1997

World History

1776	The Declaration of Independence is signed.
1789	The French Revolution begins.
1865	The American Civil War ends.
1914	World War I breaks out.
1917	The Bolshevik Revolution brings Communism to Russia.
1929	Worldwide economic depression begins.
1939	World War II begins, following the German invasion of Poland.
1957	The Vietnam War starts.
1989	The Berlin Wall is torn down, as Communism crumbles in Eastern Europe.
1996	Bill Clinton reelected U.S. president.

Fast Facts

Official name: Republic of Albania

Capital: Tiranë

Official Language: Albanian

Flag of Albania

Official religion:	None
National anthem:	"Hymni I Flamurit," meaning "hymn to the flag"
Government:	Unitary multiparty republic with one legislative house
Chief of state:	President
Head of government:	Prime minister
Area and dimensions:	The country covers 11,000 square miles (28,500 sq km). Albania's greatest distance north-south is 215 miles (346 km) and east-west is 90 miles (145 km).
Bordering countries:	Albania is bordered by Yugoslavia to the north, Macedonia (a former Yugoslav republic) to the east, Greece to the south, and the Adriatic and Ionian Seas to the west.
Highest elevation:	Mount Korab, 9,025 feet (2,751 m)
Lowest elevation:	Sea level, along the western coast

Average temperatures:

	in July	in January
Tiranë:	75°F (24°C)	44°F (7°C)

Average annual rainfall:

Tiranë:	54 inches (137 cm)

National population: (1996) 3,429,000

Sali Berisha

Roman architecture in Durrës

Populations of largest cities in Albania:	
Tiranë	300,200
Durrës	85,400
Elbasan	83,300
Shkodër	81,900
Vlorë	73,800

Famous landmarks:

▶ The Roman amphitheater in Durrës is the largest in the Balkans.

▶ Butrint, south of Sarandë, is the site of an ancient Greek colony originally settled in the sixth century B.C. The town gradually grew and became a fortified trading city. Today, you can visit the remains of the fortress, the city walls, and the baths.

▶ Rozafat Castle in Shkodër was originally built by the Illyrians.

▶ Skenderbeg's citadel in Krujë has an excellent historical museum.

▶ The fourteenth-century citadel in Gjirokastër now houses the National Museum of Arms, which has an extensive cannon collection.

▶ Muzeu Onufri in Berat is renowned for its collection of sixteenth-century religious icons and paintings.

Industry: Construction is the fastest growing sector of Albania's small industrial output. The country produces much cement and brick, as well as textiles and fertilizers. Albania's chief agricultural products are wheat, corn, potatoes, sugar beets, and olives. Albania is one of the world's leading producers of chromite. Other important mining products in Albania are petroleum, coal, and copper.

Skenderbeg Museum

Currency: The basic unit of Albanian currency is the lek, which is divided into 100 qindars. 1997 exchange rate: US$1=99.3 lekë

Weights and measures: Metric system

Literacy: 91.8%

Common Albanian words:

bajraktar	clan chieftain
besa	word of honor
breg	shore
çukë	peak
fis	clan
han	inn
kahun	legal code
katund	village
kuvendi	councils of large clans
liqen	lake
lum	river
mal	mountain
mikprites	hospitality
qytete	town
rrethe	district
urë	bridge

Elbasan

To Find Out More

Nonfiction

▶ Lear, Aaron E. *Albania*. New York: Chelsea House, 1987.

▶ Lerner Geography Department Staff. *Albania in Pictures*. Minneapolis: Lerner Publications, 1995.

Biography

▶ Clucas, Joan. *Mother Teresa*. New York: Chelsea House, 1988.

▶ Stewart, Gail B. *Alexander the Great*. San Diego: Lucent Books, 1994.

▶ Green, Robert. *Alexander the Great*. Danbury, CT: Franklin Watts, 1996.

Reference

▶ Dawson, Peter, Andrea Dawson, and Linda White. *Albania: A Guide and Illustrated Journal*. Old Saybrook, CT: Globe Pequot Press, 1995.

▶ Federal Research Division, Library of Congress. *Albania: A Country Study*. Lanham, MD: Bernam Press, 1994.

▶ Kadare, Ismail. *Albanian Spring*. New York: New Amsterdam Books, 1994.

▶ Kaplan, Robert D. *Balkan Ghosts: A Journey Through History*. New York: St. Martin's Press, 1993.

Websites

▶ **Alb Publishing**
http://www.albania.co.uk/resources/
Provides information about travel, history, and sports in Albania, as well as photographs of Albania and an Albanian folk song.

▶ **Albanian Home Page**
http://www.albanian.com/main/
Provides the latest news about Albania, information about Albanian culture, a small English-Albanian dictionary, and maps of the Balkans.

▶ **United Nations Program Office in Albania**
http://www.tirana.al/
Reports on United Nations programs in Albania.

Organizations and Embassies

▶ **Albanian Embassy**
1511 K Street NW
Washington, DC 20005
(202) 223-4942

▶ **Albanian American Cultural Foundation**
885 2nd Avenue
New York, NY 10017
(212) 207-9893

Index

Page numbers in *italics* indicate illustrations

Meet the Author

David K. Wright was born and grew up in Richmond, Indiana. He has worked for more than ten years as a reporter, copy editor, and editor for various newspapers, including the *Chicago Tribune* and the *Monroe* (Wisconsin) *Evening Times*. He has also worked as a photographer.

As for this book, he says, "I was eager to write a book about Albania, but probably for the wrong reason. There was plenty of information about every country in Europe except Albania. Why was that? I had to find out."

"When I began the book, only relatives of Albanians citizens were being admitted to the country. Since I'm not of Albanian descent, I could not travel there. There weren't many current books or articles either, so I spent time with the Albanian-American community in Boston. I also spoke with people of Albanian heritage who live in places like Detroit, Michigan; Kenosha, Wisconsin; and suburban New York City. And, of course, I used the Internet and spent long hours at local libraries."

David K. Wright lives in Madison, Wisconsin. He has written thirty-five books on subjects from the Vietnam War to Harley-Davidson motorcycles.

Photo Credits

Photographs ©: